THE MISPLACED RAPTURE

RICHARD E. SNOWDON

THE MISPLACED RAPTURE

RICHARD E. SNOWDON

AMBASSADOR INTERNATIONAL
GREENVILLE, SOUTH CAROLINA & BELFAST, NORTHERN IRELAND

www.ambassador-international.com

The Misplaced Rapture

ISBN: 978-1-62020-793-2
eISBN: 978-1-62020-792-5

Printed in UK

Ambassador International
Emerald House
427 Wade Hampton Blvd
Greenville, SC 29609, USA
www.ambassador-international.com

Ambassador Books and Media
The Mount
2 Woodstock Link
Belfast, BT6 8DD, Northern Ireland, UK
www.ambassadormedia.co.uk

The author can be contacted at the following e-mail address:
resnowdon58@gmail.com

CONTENTS

INTRODUCTION

Not a Christian yet?

This book has been written primarily for those who are already Christians. If the reader is unsure of where he or she stands with God, or professes no faith at all, Appendix 1 should be read carefully before attempting the rest of the book. It contains a brief explanation of mankind's true history, the origin of sin and its presence in every person upon earth. The Gospel (or *good news*) of God's grace in the Lord Jesus Christ is shown to be the *only* way of salvation from sin's penalty and power. The reader is urged to be reconciled to God by believing the Gospel without delay because, whether conscious of it or not, time is fast running out.

A clear warning needs to be sounded in these days of 'easy believism', particularly in the West. There are a great many within the professing church who would call themselves Christians and imagine that they have been 'born-again' after responding to some emotional appeal, often at a hyped-up meeting. Perhaps you have repeated some formula-prayer (sometimes known as 'the sinner's prayer') and then been assured that you are now saved. Dear reader, please be very careful here. True saving faith is a deep work of the Holy Spirit. He convinces and convicts us of the sin and rebellion in our hearts against God and enables us to be willing to turn away from it and trust in the Lord Jesus Christ for the forgiveness of our sins. True conversion will always be marked by a radical change in the direction of our lives. It involves a very definite departure from all known sin and handing over the lordship of our lives from ourselves to Jesus. The real Jesus of the Bible died on the cross bearing our sins and was raised from the dead on the third day. To the true convert He becomes both Lord and Saviour. Please do not be taken in by the popular, 'touchy-feely' 'Jesus' who comes to improve your self-esteem, fix your relationships or make you successful in your career. If an outsider would find your life indistinguishable from your unsaved family, friends and neighbours, then the likelihood is that you are not truly a child of God.

Sleeping Churches

The author also recognises that many Christians have adopted a nonliteral approach to Bible prophecy. This is most often the result of subscribing to a theological system known as 'Amillennialism'. The word 'Amillennialism' simply means 'no millennium'. Its teaching denies that there will be a literal 1000 year reign of Christ on Earth, despite being told that there will be, with the phrase *"a* [or the] *thousand years"* being repeated six times in six consecutive verses in Revelation chapter 20. A major handicap of this system is its failure to distinguish between God's separate purposes for national Israel and those for the Church, resulting in what has become known as 'Replacement Theology'. The 'Replacement' here refers to the erroneous belief that the Church has entirely replaced the nation of Israel in God's purposes. Such a belief inevitably leads to spiritual blindness concerning the significance of the many clearly prophesied signs of the end of this present Age, which are now escalating daily. The greatest of these is the fact that Israel now exists as a nation again after nearly 2000 years of dispersion throughout the world. It is not within the scope of this book to undertake a thorough refutation of Amillennialism.

However, I would strongly encourage the reader to search these things out for themselves in the Scriptures, rather than allowing a system to tell you what to believe. Consider the fact that the many prophecies of Christ's First Coming were fulfilled *literally*. This caused Israel's religious leadership to stumble in their spiritual blindness, which was the result of adherence to their man-made and corrupt religious system. Likewise, many Christians are likely to be taken completely by surprise when the Lord Jesus comes to catch up His Bride to the place that He has prepared for her in Heaven. What warrant do we have for failing to take the prophecies of the Rapture, the Tribulation to follow and Christ's Second Coming *literally?*

Leaving aside the false teachings of Roman Catholicism and liberal Protestantism, another major problem within the professing church is the increasing number of leaders who are encouraging each other and their membership not to be concerned with teaching Bible prophecy. Incredibly, this is being done in the name of 'church growth', with claims that the youth of today will be 'put off' by the teaching of prophecy. On the contrary, as a street preacher, this author has had many conversations with thoughtful young people, some of whom sense that something big is afoot in the world. They want and deserve credible answers to their questions, which can only be given if one has an accurate understanding of Bible prophecy. Understanding that the Rapture is imminent and unlikely to be delayed much longer, is a powerful incentive for young people not to put off getting right with God and for believers to wake up and shake off the shackles of lukewarm profession and worldliness.

Then there are those churches and ministries that do understand the vital importance of Bible prophecy, but have misunderstood the purpose for God's timing of the Rapture and insist that the Church must go through part or all of the seven year Tribulation period. Simple logic enables one to see that this sort of teaching automatically removes any hope of an imminent appearing of the Lord Jesus Christ, along with the powerful, sanctifying influence that such an understanding is divinely calculated to bring. That brings us to the main purpose for writing this book.

Our Blessed Hope

Attacks on the "*blessed hope*" held out by the Word of God to all true Christians are nothing new. What *is* new, is the dramatic escalation in their frequency and, sadly, the wrong spirit in which some of these attacks are made.

Many of God's people have been too easily robbed of the comfort that the "*blessed hope*" is well calculated to give, by our tendency to put mere men and their teachings upon pedestals. A man might have a glowing reputation for the faithful teaching of God's Word and yet be blind or in error over an important issue.

What is this "*blessed hope*" and what makes it so particularly *blessed?*

> *Looking for* ***that blessed hope,*** *and the glorious appearing of the great God and our Saviour Jesus Christ;* *(Titus 2:13)*

Let us ask two vital questions. As we approach the end of the Age, can it really be a light matter that so many Christians appear to have no awareness of the signs of the times or their immense significance? Of those believers who do understand that we are clearly living in the End Times, can it be a matter of little consequence that so many have no idea whether to expect to see the Lord Jesus Christ or the Antichrist first? Titus 2:13 and many verses like it are unambiguous in instructing us as to what, or rather *Who*, we should be looking for.

Rather than accepting the current status quo, which is a hotchpotch of contradictory notions concerning the timing of the Rapture or even denial that it will occur at all, as faithful disciples of the Lord Jesus Christ we should be insisting upon the *truth.* Why? Firstly because Jesus Christ *is the truth* and secondly the Holy Spirit has been given to *guide us into* ***all*** *truth.* God has given us His entire counsel in the Bible and the glory of His Name is vitally connected with it. What can be said of our discipleship if we are indifferent as to whether our beliefs about weighty matters such as the Rapture are actually *true* or not? Are we *really* concerned about and jealous for God's glory to the extent that we simply *must* have the truth and cannot be contented with the prevailing and confused *views of men?*

A careful examination of *all* the scriptures relating to the return of the Lord Jesus Christ will reveal that there is a distinct difference between Christ's coming for His Bride (the true Church) at what many call the Rapture and His Second Advent in glory at the end of the seven year Tribulation period. See Appendix 2 for the relevant scriptures conveniently tabulated for comparison.

Paul urged Timothy to:

> *Study to shew thyself approved unto God, a workman that needeth not to be ashamed, rightly dividing the word of truth.* (2 Timothy 2:15)

After giving serious thought to the warning given in James 3:1 that, because of stricter judgement criteria, not many should become teachers, if we really are called to teach the Word of God, then we must be those who are *"rightly dividing the word of truth"*. It has been pointed out that when Jesus Christ was on Earth, the Jewish religious leaders failed to *rightly divide* their own scriptures which portrayed the Messiah as both a suffering servant and conquering King. Similarly, many with teaching ministries within the Church are not *"rightly dividing"* scriptures relating to the Second Coming, resulting in a failure to distinguish between the Rapture of the Church and the Second Advent of the Lord Jesus Christ in power and glory at the end of the seven year Tribulation. It is vital, when reading the Scriptures, to determine *to* whom the passage is written and *about* whom it is written. Failure in this respect leads to applying wrong scriptures to wrong groups of people resulting in wrong doctrine. I am convinced and saddened that many reputable Bible teachers who deny a pre-Tribulation Rapture will be very red-faced at the imminent and soon coming appearance of the Lord Jesus Christ for His Church.

Many scholarly books have been written, both yesteryear and more recently, that demonstrate beyond all reasonable doubt, *from the Scriptures*, that the Lord Jesus will descend from Heaven to catch away the true Church to Heaven before God's wrath is poured out upon this world. Therefore it is not my primary intention to write yet another book proving the truth of the pre-Tribulation Rapture. Rather, I have a twofold aim. The first is to encourage Christians who have always rejoiced in this "*blessed hope*" but have become confused and discouraged by the increasing number in ministry lining up to deny it. Let us always remember that the ultimate truth of a matter is determined by the Scriptures *alone* and not by any speaker or preacher, no matter in what esteem they are held. Secondly I hope to make it obvious *why*, at this critical juncture in world history, there is such an escalating attack on the pre-Tribulation Rapture.

After looking at what it means to *rightly divide* the Word of God and examining the roots of Rapture confusion, we will take a look at many of the points and objections raised by those who deny a pre-Tribulation Rapture and subject them to a close scriptural scrutiny. In seeking to answer their arguments, it is hoped that the reader will begin to comprehend the underlying leaven and faulty theology that underpins these attacks. The principle adopted throughout will be that if our understanding of any particular matter is correct then, by definition, it cannot and will not contradict any scriptures at all. Conversely, if we have a wrong understanding of a matter, it may seem to find support in isolated scriptures (usually taken out of context) but it will inevitably unravel when the whole counsel of God is taken into account.

Next we will examine some of the beautiful 'types and shadows' of the Hebrew Scriptures (Old Testament) that wonderfully foreshadow the New Testament pattern of a pre-Tribulation Rapture. Although we do not take our doctrine from 'types and shadows', we are warranted to look for them *after* we have accurately established the truth from the New Testament. Many, including this author, can testify to the thrill and delight of finding these 'types and shadows', which God clearly placed in His Word for a purpose. What was that purpose? Surely it was for the edification and encouragement of His future saints who would understand these truths from the clear revelation in the New Testament. Can it really be without significance that there are *no* types and shadows that lend themselves to supporting a mid or post-Tribulation Rapture pattern? Perhaps not surprisingly, many who deny a pre-Tribulation Rapture tend to downplay this lovely feature of the Hebrew Scriptures.

We will then dwell briefly on the widespread expectations

of those immersed in today's New Age and UFO cults. Why are we doing this? Is it because our doctrine should be in any way influenced by their teachings? By no means! However, having carefully established the truth from the Word of God, it is most interesting and not at all surprising to find that Satan, through these false movements, has been busy constructing a counterfeit explanation for the sudden, mass disappearance of millions of people from the face of the planet. This is precisely what we would expect if the Rapture is to occur before the seven year Tribulation period. Clearly, if those who teach a post-Tribulation Rapture were correct, this interesting observation would make no sense at all.

Finally, we will seek to answer the vitally important question: which of the various contradictory teachings concerning the Rapture timing glorifies God?

CHAPTER 1

RIGHTLY DIVIDING THE WORD OF GOD

When faced with a slick, 'rapid-fire' presentation that aims to persuade you that the Lord Jesus Christ could not come for His Church at any moment, it can be very difficult to assess the scriptural validity of a statement or quote before the next point has been made.

The aim of this chapter is to slow things right down and take a brief look at underlying principles that aid us in rightly dividing the word of God. To help us keep our thinking on track whilst considering these matters, two points that we might call 'Golden Keys' should be borne in mind:

1. Prophetic passages in Scripture should always be interpreted literally unless the context clearly indicates that 'picture language' is being used. In such cases, the picture or symbol used will be interpreted elsewhere in the same passage or in another part of Scripture.

2. The Church of Jesus Christ is not mentioned in the Hebrew Scriptures (Old Testament). It is a 'mystery' not revealed until the time of the New Covenant Apostles and Prophets.
   (Romans 16:25-27; Ephesians 3:2-13; Colossians 1:26)

Many opponents of the pre-Tribulation Rapture would generally hold to the first of these 'Golden Keys' but, as we shall see in chapters 3 and 4, regularly ignore the vital principle of the second key. So how can we ensure that we correctly apply the principle of the second key?

When reading any passage of Scripture, it is vital to ask the following questions. *To whom* is the passage written? *About whom* is the passage written? As we said in the Introduction, failure in this respect leads to applying wrong scriptures to wrong groups of people resulting in wrong doctrine.

A passage might be written to the same people to whom it concerns. Alternatively, it could be written to one people group about another people group. It is overly simplistic and not strictly accurate to make a statement such as, "The Hebrew Scriptures are all about Israel and the New Testament is all about the Church". Let us have a look at some examples from the Old and New Testaments that demonstrate the fallacy of such a simplistic statement.

The first eleven chapters of Genesis up until the call of Abraham, though obviously part of the Hebrew Scriptures, are not about Israel since she did not yet exist. Similarly, the book of Job, though part of the Hebrew Scriptures, has nothing to do with Israel. The Hebrew prophets, though primarily concerned with God's dealings with Israel, sometimes spoke about other nations and peoples.

> ***The burden of Egypt.*** *Behold, the LORD rideth upon a swift cloud, and shall come into Egypt: and the idols of Egypt shall be moved at his presence, and the heart of Egypt shall melt in the midst of it.* (Isaiah 19:1)

> *The word that the LORD spake* ***against Babylon*** *and against* ***the land of the Chaldeans*** *by Jeremiah the prophet.* (Jeremiah 50:1)

> *Son of man, set thy face against Gog,* ***the land of Magog,*** *the chief prince of Meshech and Tubal, and prophesy against him,* (Ezekiel 38:2)

In these examples it is clear that the prophets are not speaking *about* Israel. However, what is said still forms part of God's Word *to* Israel. Should it therefore be a surprise to find a similar thing occurring in the New Testament?

The Lord Jesus mentioned the Gentiles many times during His ministry, at which time they were neither Israel nor a part of the Church as she had not yet been born. The apostle Paul devoted three full chapters, Romans chapters 9, 10 and 11, to explaining the truth *about* Israel *to* the Church. Furthermore he wrote the following *to* the Church *about* the Hebrew Scriptures:

> *For whatsoever things were written* ***aforetime*** *were written for our learning, that we through patience and comfort of the scriptures might have hope.* (Romans 15:4)

The Hebrew Scriptures were neither written *to* the Church (which did not then exist) or *about* the Church (the future existence of which was completely unknown to the writers). Yet Paul tells us that it was written for *our* learning! The explanation for this is simple; God in His foreknowledge knew that He would bring the Church into existence and that the Hebrew Scriptures would provide the essential canon of truth with which to verify all of the claims of the Lord Jesus Christ and His Apostles. Indeed, the Hebrew Scriptures were the only Bible that the very early Church had. Of course it also left Israel (as represented by their corrupt religious leaders) to whom it *was* written, without excuse for rejecting their Messiah. More than this, the Hebrew Scriptures provide an exceedingly rich and indispensable mine of historical and spiritual truth. All major doctrines of the Bible have their roots in the book of Genesis; wonderful truths clearly revealed in the New Testament are very frequently discerned in the form of 'types and shadows' in the Hebrew Scriptures. An understanding of these things will guard us against the folly of thinking that we can be 'New Testament only' Christians. Speaking about the history of Israel in the Hebrew Scriptures, Paul writes the following exhortation for Christians:

> *Now these things happened unto **them** by way of example; and they were written for **our** admonition, upon whom the ends of the ages are come.*
> *(1 Corinthians 10:11 RV)*

These words, along with those previously quoted from Romans 15:4, make it very clear that, although the Hebrew Scriptures were not written *to* us, they were most certainly written *for* us. Paul sums up the whole issue very concisely in the following well-known verse:

> ***All scripture** is given by inspiration of God, and is profitable for doctrine, for reproof, for correction, for instruction in righteousness:* *(2 Timothy 3:16)*

In this verse, *"All scripture"* means exactly what it says, encompassing the entire Old and New Testaments.

When reading the Gospels, there is a tendency to forget that the Church was not in existence for almost all of the time period that they cover; she was not born until after the resurrection of the Lord Jesus from the dead. Taking into account God's foreknowledge that Israel would, through unbelief, reject her Messiah, the period of the Gospels can be viewed legitimately as part of a transition phase from one dispensation to another. Although the Lord Jesus had made a very brief mention of building His Church in

Matthew 16:18, He did not enlarge upon it or give any clear doctrinal instruction concerning it at that point. It is clear that the disciples still had little understanding of what the Church was to be even after the Resurrection. Just before His Ascension we find them still concerned with the restoration of the kingdom to Israel (Acts 1:6). It must be emphasised that this was an entirely legitimate concern but, nonetheless, showed that they had no real grasp of what the Church was to be at this stage.

CHAPTER 2

THE ROOT OF RAPTURE CONFUSION

One cannot be long involved in studying the timing of the Rapture without noting the heavy reliance placed upon such passages as Matthew chapter 24 by those denying that it will occur before the Tribulation. There seems to be an almost unquestioned assumption that wherever such expressions as *"the elect"* or *"the saints"* are used, they must of necessity be referring to the Church. However, is this justified?

A simple analogy might be helpful here. In the past, when *all* tables were made of wood, does it necessarily follow that *all* wood was therefore a table? The logical fallacy of this is easy to see and the answer is obviously no. In like manner, it is absolutely correct to say that the true Church is composed entirely of saints. Does this mean that all saints must therefore be part of the Church? Again, the answer to this is definitely no. By applying the principle of our second 'Golden Key' (mentioned at the beginning of chapter 1), wherever words such as *"saint"* or *"elect"* are used in the Hebrew Scriptures (Old Testament), we can be sure that neither the writer nor the reader would perceive that some of these references *might* include Church saints. Of course, God in His foreknowledge would know that the saints referred to in Zechariah 14:5, for example, would include Church saints. However, the future existence of the Church was at that time a mystery, not yet revealed. The important point to remember is that there are *"saints"* or *"elect"* who are not a part of the Church.

Bearing all this in mind, we are now ready to consider whether words such as "*saint*" and "*elect*", when used in the New Testament, must *automatically* refer to the Church. Since it is so frequently referred to by those denying a pre-Tribulation Rapture, we will take Matthew chapter 24 as an example.

> *(Matthew 24:15) When ye therefore shall see the abomination of desolation, spoken of by Daniel the prophet, stand in the holy place, (whoso readeth, let him understand:)*
>
> *(Matthew 24:16) Then let them which be* ***in Judaea*** *flee into the mountains:*
>
> *(Matthew 24:17) Let him which is on the housetop not come down to take any thing out of his house:*
>
> *(Matthew 24:18) Neither let him which is in the field return back to take his clothes.*
>
> *(Matthew 24:19) And woe unto them that are with child, and to them that give suck in those days!*
>
> *(Matthew 24:20) But pray ye that your flight be not in the winter, neither* ***on the sabbath day:***
>
> *(Matthew 24:21) For* ***then shall be great tribulation,*** *such as was not since the beginning of the world to this time, no, nor ever shall be.*
>
> *(Matthew 24:22) And except those days should be shortened, there should no flesh be saved: but for* ***the elect's*** *sake those days shall be shortened.*

Most are agreed that Jesus is here dealing with the Tribulation period. However, at issue is the vital matter of just *who* He is giving commands to. It must be remembered that Jesus was addressing the disciples whose thoughts, at this point, were centred on Israel and who had no clear understanding of what the coming Church was to be. Notice that His instructions are very narrowly defined geographically and are distinctly Jewish in character. Some insist that these directions are given to that part of the Church that finds itself in Judaea. However, since when has the Church been subject to the ordinance of the Sabbath (verse 20)? Moreover, why would they be the only Christians in the world needing special direction from God at this critical point in the Tribulation? The difficulty is entirely removed if one realises that Jesus is speaking *about* and *to* the faithful remnant of Israel who will be 'centre stage' in the Tribulation period. This understanding is further confirmed by a close study of Revelation chapter 12.

> *And there appeared a great wonder in heaven;* ***a woman clothed with the sun,*** *and the moon under her feet, and upon her head a crown of twelve stars:* (Revelation 12:1)

It is vitally important to identify correctly who the "*woman clothed with the sun*" represents. There have been many false interpretations. The Roman Catholic Church identifies her as Mary. Many Protestant denominations identify her as the Church throughout the ages. However, as always, the Bible is its own best interpreter. The "*woman*" is associated with the sun, moon and stars. When we search the Scriptures concerning this we find a very adequate solution to the enigma in one of Joseph's dreams in the book of Genesis.

> (Genesis 37:9) *And he dreamed yet another dream, and told it his brethren, and said, Behold, I have dreamed a dream more; and, behold,* ***the sun and the moon and the eleven stars*** *made obeisance to me.*

> *(Genesis 37:10) And he told it to his father, and to his brethren: and his father rebuked him, and said unto him, What is this dream that thou hast dreamed?* ***Shall I and thy mother and thy brethren*** *indeed come to bow down ourselves to thee to the earth?*

From this account we can see that Jacob had no problem in understanding what Joseph's dream represented. Notice that only eleven stars are mentioned in the dream, but twelve stars comprise the crown in Revelation 12:1. Why is this? The answer is that Joseph himself is the twelfth star. Therefore the "*woman clothed with the sun*" unquestionably represents the nation of Israel, which descended from the twelve sons of Jacob. With this in mind, let us return to Revelation chapter 12 and find a remarkable correlation with Matthew 24:16.

> *And* ***the woman fled into the wilderness,*** *where she hath a place prepared of God, that they should feed her there* ***a thousand two hundred and threescore days*** **[3½ years].** *(Revelation 12:6)*

> *And to* ***the woman*** *were given two wings of a great eagle,* ***that she might fly into the wilderness,*** *into her place, where she is nourished for* ***a time, and times, and half a time*** **[3½ years]**, *from the face of the serpent. (Revelation 12:14)*

> *Then let* ***them which be in Judaea flee into the mountains:*** *(Matthew 24:16)*

In Revelation 12:6 and 12:14, we find "*the woman*" (Israel) fleeing into the wilderness for 3½ years to be protected by God from Satan's onslaught against them. In Matthew 24:16 we find "*them which be in Judaea*" fleeing into the mountains. Matthew 24:15 and 24:21 fix that time as being the beginning of the "*Great Tribulation*", which corresponds with the middle of Daniel's 70th *"week"* (seven year period) in Daniel 9:27. Clearly, the middle of a seven year period leaves 3½ years still to run. From this we can see that *"the woman"* of Revelation 12 and *"them which be in Judaea"* of Matthew 24 are one and the same, namely Israel.

As one continues to read up to Matthew 24:30, it is obvious that the whole context of the chapter is the Tribulation period leading up to the Lord Jesus Christ's Second Advent in glory and has nothing to do with the Rapture of the Church. Unfortunately, some who hold to the pre-Tribulation Rapture are muddying the waters by allowing that verse 31 and/or verses 40 and 41 refer to the Rapture of the Church.

> *And he shall send his angels with a great sound of a trumpet, and they shall gather together his elect from the four winds, from one end of heaven to the other. (Matthew 24:31)*

Matthew 24:31 certainly cannot describe the Rapture of the Church for a number of reasons. Firstly, the finer details of the Rapture were not revealed until many years after the Lord's Olivet discourse, when the apostle Paul made known the *mystery.*

> *Behold, I shew you* ***a mystery;*** *We shall not all sleep, but we shall all be changed, (1 Corinthians 15:51)*

A *mystery*, in the sense of the above verse, is a truth that had previously been concealed but has now been revealed. Although the Lord Jesus briefly alluded to the Rapture in John 14:3, He did not give sufficient detail for the disciples to be able to understand the staggering scope of the promised event or its chronological distinction from the Second Advent. That understanding was to come later.

Secondly, in Matthew 24:31 the *elect* are to be gathered by angelic agency. This is not the case with the Rapture of the Church, when the Lord Himself shall descend from Heaven into the air to collect His Bride.

> *For* ***the Lord himself*** *shall descend from heaven with a shout, with the voice of the archangel, and with the trump of God: and* ***the dead in Christ shall rise first:*** *(1 Thessalonians 4:16)*

Thirdly, in Matthew 24:31 there is no mention of the *dead in Christ* rising first. Is it really likely that the Lord Jesus would leave out such a stupendous detail as this? Clearly not, which is further proof that the Rapture of the Church is not in view in this verse.

However, what about verses 40 and 41, which surely paint a scenario akin to what will happen at the Rapture of the Church?

> *(Matthew 24:40) Then shall two be in the field; the one shall be taken, and the other left.*

> *(Matthew 24:41) Two women shall be grinding at the mill; the one shall be taken, and the other left.*

When trying to interpret passages such as this, *context* is all important. The 'big picture' context of the whole of Matthew 24 is that of the Tribulation period leading up to the Second Coming of the Lord Jesus Christ in power and great glory to set up His Kingdom. The immediate context of verses 40 and 41 is obtained by reading from verse 37. In this passage we find that the Lord Jesus is using the characteristics of the days leading up to and including the judgement of Noah's Flood to illustrate similarities with events leading up to and including His Second Coming in judgement.

(Matthew 24:37) But as the days of Noe were, so shall also the coming of the Son of man be.

(Matthew 24:38) For as in the days that were before the flood ***they*** *were eating and drinking, marrying and giving in marriage, until the day that Noe entered into the ark,*

(Matthew 24:39) And ***knew not*** *until the flood came, and took* ***them*** *all away; so shall also the coming of the Son of man be.*

From a careful reading of these verses, it is clear that the ones taken away by the flood were the ones carrying on the normal activities of life *("eating and drinking, marrying and giving in marriage...")* in blissful ignorance of the approaching judgement. Some have suggested that Noah and his family were the ones taken away in the safety of the Ark and that it was the unbelievers left behind. However, this cannot be, because verse 39 makes it very clear that the ones taken away were those who "***knew not*** *until the flood came*". This could not possibly be said of Noah, otherwise he would never have built the Ark!

If we now apply the Lord's reasoning to verses 40 and 41, it becomes clear that it is the unbelievers who are taken away in judgement. This also fits the overall context of Matthew 24, culminating in those who have put their faith in the Lord Jesus and physically survived the Tribulation period going through into the Millennial Kingdom. Conversely, unbelievers who have physically survived until the end of the Tribulation will be removed in judgement.

Taking all this into account, we can see that the Rapture of the Church does not feature at all in Matthew 24. Having deduced from many other scriptures that the Rapture must occur before the beginning of the seven year Tribulation period, we find that there is no contradiction to this in Matthew 24. We mentioned earlier that some who hold to the pre-Tribulation Rapture have applied Matthew 24 verses 31 and/or 40 and 41 to this event. If they really did represent the Rapture, they would certainly cast doubt on it taking place before the Tribulation! We need to be extremely careful not to misapply scriptures in support of our case. Overall, the conclusion of the Matthew 24 issue is that it is not about the Church at all and that trying to force the Church into it is bound to produce confusion at best and wrong doctrine at worst.

Here we must pause briefly, before proceeding further, to anticipate the indignation with which our conclusion is likely to be met in some quarters. "You cannot carve up the Word of God like that, declaring that some parts are about the Church and others are not" will come the cry. To which we reply that we have a divine warrant for *rightly* 'carving up' the Scriptures! When we carve a joint of meat we are, by definition, *dividing* it.

> *Study to shew thyself approved unto God, a workman that needeth not to be ashamed,* ***rightly dividing the word of truth.*** *(2 Timothy 2:15)*

In this verse, Paul's instructions to Timothy make it very clear that dividing the Word of God is an absolute necessity. However, we are to *rightly* divide the Word, not arbitrarily according to our own whim and fancy. This can only be achieved by studying the Word diligently, to show ourselves *"approved unto God"*. I believe it can also be deduced from this verse that many *'workmen'* will *"be ashamed"* over error they have taught, when the Lord Jesus returns for His Church. I further believe that a failure to prepare God's people for the *imminent* return of the Lord Jesus will be prominent among those errors.

THE STRUCTURE OF THE BOOK OF REVELATION

It is highly significant that after Revelation chapter 3 the Church is not referred to as being on Earth until, in chapter 19, she is seen (in Heaven) preparing herself to accompany the Lord Jesus Christ back to Earth at His Second Advent. Clearly, she must have been removed from the Earth at some point prior to this. Chapter 4 opens in a most interesting way:

> *After this I looked, and, behold, a door was opened in heaven: and the first voice which I heard was as it were of a trumpet talking with me; which said,* ***Come up hither,*** *and I will shew thee things which must be hereafter.* (*Revelation 4:1*)

Many have seen in John's being caught up into Heaven an allusion to the Rapture of the Church. In view of the fact that she is not seen on Earth again until the end of chapter 19, this is not unreasonable.

Objectors will point out that the word *"saints"* occurs several times between chapters 4 and 18 and insist that this is clear proof that the Church is on Earth throughout the Tribulation. We would just remind the reader of the analogy used earlier in this chapter, where we used simple logic to conclude that if all tables were made of wood, it does not necessarily follow that all wood must therefore be a table! Likewise, not all saints are part of the Church. However, more potently than that, the Scriptures are so exquisitely accurate that where something that we might humanly expect to find in a passage is omitted, there is a very good reason for it. Examples of this can be found in other parts of Scripture. In Luke 4:18-19 the Lord Jesus read from Isaiah 61:1-2 but omitted the last part of verse 2 that says *"the day of vengeance of our God"*. That is because that aspect of Isaiah's prophecy is connected with Jesus' Second Coming and not His First. So we see that an omission can be very important.

CHAPTER 3

DEALING WITH OBJECTIONS (PART 1)

In this chapter we shall examine some of the points made and objections raised by those who teach that the Lord Jesus Christ could not come for His Church at any moment. These points have been collated after painstakingly going through videos and recordings of a few well-known speakers who insist that the Church must go through some or all of the Tribulation, thereby destroying the doctrine of imminence. Some, realising that 'imminence' is at the heart of the issue, have sought to make a direct attack upon it, as we shall see in objection number 10. The list is not intended to be exhaustive, but aims to deal with the most commonly encountered objections. It is hoped that by studying the Word thoroughly for themselves, readers will be able to identify the logical fallacies and/or misuse of Scripture inherent in any other opposing arguments. The different contentions are numbered for convenience of reference, with the rebuttal or answer following each point.

1. The word *Rapture* does not appear in the Bible.

Answer: Neither do the words *Trinity* or *Bible!* It does not bode well for the rest of a message when this is the opening argument. The word *Rapture* is simply used to describe an event that *is* clearly defined in Scripture. One could just as easily describe it as the *Translation* of the Church or the

Catching Away of the Church. For the record, the Latin word "*Rapiemur*" from which we derive our English word *Rapture* ***is*** in the Latin Vulgate translation of the Bible and is the word used in 1 Thessalonians 4:17 to translate the Greek word "*Harpazo*". The Strong's definition of the Greek word "*Harpazo*" is as follows: *to seize (in various applications): - catch (away, up), pluck, pull, take (by force).* Clearly, one does not need to be a Greek scholar to see that this objection carries no weight.

2. The doctrine of the Rapture was invented by John Nelson Darby after listening to the ecstatic utterances of a woman named Margaret MacDonald in the 1830s.

Answer: The best indicator of the invalidity of this objection is the fact that so many highly respected Bible teachers have demonstrated the truth of a pre-Tribulation Rapture from the Scriptures *alone.* They have neither desired, much less needed, an extra-biblical source to corroborate the clear teaching of Scripture.

This constantly repeated allegation is disingenuous at best and dishonest at worst. Its purpose is to persuade the enquirer that the doctrine of the pre-Tribulation Rapture is not obtained from the Scriptures, but outside of them. This issue has been dealt with exhaustively by various authors who have investigated the matter in depth. Interestingly, there exists a quote by a Syrian theologian called Ephraem from around 373 AD, which is an extremely clear statement of his belief in a pre-Tribulation Rapture of the Church. This belief clearly existed a very long time before the supposed 'new revelation' of Margaret MacDonald in the 1830s! Yet the supreme irony of this objection becomes clear if one takes the trouble to actually read Margaret MacDonald's 'utterance'. Amongst other things, she envisages the true Church being opposed by the Antichrist which, far from pointing to a pre-Tribulation Rapture, places the Church in the Tribulation period; hardly an auspicious foundation on which to build the doctrine of the pre-Tribulation Rapture!

3. Those who believe the pre-Tribulation Rapture doctrine are simply wanting to escape trials and persecution. Jesus said in John 16:33 that in the world we would have tribulation.

Answer: This is just a straightforward case of not understanding the difference between the general trials and tribulations that have been the lot of true Christians throughout the last 2000 years and the very specific, yet future, seven year period called *The* Tribulation. Many Christians have suffered terrible persecutions and cruel martyrdoms in various parts of the world throughout the whole of Church history. In our own country, faithful men such as Cranmer, Latimer and Ridley were burnt at the stake by the Roman Catholic Church in the 1550s. As I write, many Christians throughout the world are suffering severe persecution under Islam and other oppressive regimes. Yet none of these were in *The* Tribulation period. Further to this, the seven year Tribulation period is synonymous with Daniel's 70th week:

> *Seventy weeks are determined* ***upon thy people*** *and upon thy holy city, to finish the transgression, and to make an end of sins, and to make reconciliation for iniquity, and to bring in everlasting righteousness, and to seal up the vision and prophecy, and to anoint the most Holy.* (Daniel 9:24)

It is vital to understand that these 70 weeks (or 'sevens') of years specifically concern Daniel's people, i.e. the Jews. Another verse from the Hebrew Scriptures (Old Testament) makes it abundantly clear which group of people this future seven year period is focused on:

> *Alas! for that day is great, so that none is like it: it is even* ***the time of Jacob's trouble;*** *but he shall be saved out of it.* *(Jeremiah 30:7)*

Again, the reference here to Jacob makes it very clear that the nation of Israel is in view. Using the second of the 'Golden Keys' mentioned at the beginning of chapter 1, we can very safely deduce that this has nothing whatsoever to do with the Church. Neither Daniel nor Jeremiah knew anything about a future Church and indeed she is not mentioned anywhere else in the Hebrew Scriptures. If the Church did not exist and therefore did not feature in the first 69 weeks of Daniel's prophecy, why should she suddenly appear in the 70th? Indeed, the Hebrew prophets foresaw this future seven year period in considerable detail. Is it really likely that they would have failed to notice a very large body of mainly Gentile believers sharing the scene with Israel?

One speaker recently made an illuminating observation. He said that, by placing the Church into a period that concerns only the Jewish nation, we are guilty of a kind of 'Reverse Replacement Theology'. By this he meant that, instead of erroneously teaching that the Church has replaced Israel (Replacement Theology), the opposite error is taught in which the Church is forced into a distinct period of future history (Daniel's 70th week) that concerns only Israel*. Perhaps we could refer to this error as 'Gatecrasher Theology'!

(This is not to imply that all the other nations of the world*

are exempt from this awesome outpouring of God's wrath. On the contrary, the whole world will experience God's judgement during Daniel's 70th week.)

4. There is not a single verse in the Scriptures saying that the Rapture must occur before the Tribulation.

Answer: It is remarkable how often this objection is woven into arguments against a pre-Tribulation Rapture. Remarkable, because important biblical doctrines are not always clearly enunciated in a single verse. Rather, they are obtained by a prayerful and thorough comparison of scripture with scripture and, above all, *"rightly dividing the Word of Truth"*. No true believer would demand a totally comprehensive scriptural proof of the doctrine of the Trinity in a single verse. That is the sort of demand that a Jehovah's Witness would make on the doorstep of a Christian or that Muslims often make of street preachers concerning the deity of the Lord Jesus Christ.

> *Study to shew thyself approved unto God, a workman that needeth not to be ashamed,* ***rightly dividing the word of truth.*** *(2 Timothy 2:15)*

The above injunction by the apostle Paul would be totally unnecessary if the Holy Spirit intended us to be able to demonstrate all Bible doctrines by simply quoting a single verse.

Ironically, there is no *single* verse proving that the Church *does* go through part or all of the Tribulation!

However, having highlighted how unreasonable is the demand to prove the doctrine of the pre-Tribulation Rapture in a single verse, there are verses which do just that.

*Because **thou** hast kept the word of my patience, I also will **keep thee from the hour of temptation**, which shall come upon all **the world**, to try **them** that dwell upon the earth.* (Revelation 3:10)

In this wonderful promise to the Philadelphian Church, the Lord Jesus Christ makes a clear distinction between His people and the people of the world along with their entirely different destinies. The "*hour of temptation*" is a clear reference to the Tribulation period. Since that did not occur whilst any of the Philadelphian believers were still alive, it is clear that the promise applies to all faithful Christians throughout the Church Age. To be 'kept from' the Tribulation means exactly what it says, namely that the true Church will not be present on the Earth during the entirety of that period. This is perfectly in keeping with both the character of God and all other scriptures relating to the issue. It surely takes a determination to twist the straightforward meaning out of this verse in order to make it mean anything else.

*...and to wait for his Son from heaven, whom he raised from the dead, even Jesus, which **delivereth us from the wrath to come**.* (1 Thessalonians 1:10 RV)

Here again, it is extremely clear that Jesus will deliver all true Christians from the "*wrath to come*". Some have tried to insinuate that the wrath mentioned here is a reference to Hell and not the coming seven year Tribulation. This cannot be, because the context of the verse has to do with waiting for the coming of the Lord Jesus to receive us unto Himself and thus deliver us from the wrath about to be visited by God upon the world.

*For God hath **not appointed us to wrath**, but to obtain salvation by our Lord Jesus Christ,* (1 Thessalonians 5:9)

Once more we have a clear reference to promised deliverance for God's children from the wrath to come. The obvious implication of these verses and their correspondence with the overall scriptural principle that God delivers the righteous from His judgements, has led Satan to resort to an ingenious sleight of hand. He has managed to persuade some that the seven year Tribulation is all about his wrath, not God's wrath! This is the subject of the next objection and, as we shall see, is blatantly unscriptural.

5. The Tribulation is Satan's wrath; the "Day of the Lord" (God's wrath) is not until the end of the Tribulation.

Answer: A careful study of the book of Revelation (and other related scriptures) would prevent believers from being led astray by such assertions. Not only that, but a blessing is promised to all who read or hear the Revelation and keep hold of its message.

> *Blessed is he that readeth, and they that hear the words of this prophecy, and keep those things which are written therein: for the time is at hand.* (Revelation 1:3)

The first thing to say is that the Tribulation itself and the entirety of events within it are under the total control of the Lord Jesus Christ, not Satan.

> *And I saw when* ***the Lamb opened*** *one of* ***the seals,*** *and I heard, as it were the noise of thunder, one of the four beasts saying, Come and see.* (Revelation 6:1)

To attribute the Tribulation period to Satan's wrath is like putting Israel's Babylonian captivity down to Nebuchadnezzar's wrath. Clearly, the Babylonian captivity was God's chastisement of His people for their continued idolatry and sin after many warnings. God planned and controlled the exact day on which it would start and its precise duration. Nebuchadnezzar was merely a tool in God's hand. Similarly, Satan and his Antichrist are mere tools that God will use to fulfil His purposes in judging this evil and Christ-rejecting world.

If we want to know whose wrath the Tribulation is all about, we only have to read to the end of the same chapter.

> *(Revelation 6:16) And said to the mountains and rocks, Fall on us, and hide us from the face of him that sitteth on the throne, and from* ***the wrath of the Lamb:***

> *(Revelation 6:17) For* ***the great day of his wrath*** *is come; and who shall be able to stand?*

It is clear from these verses that the opening of the seals, which is entirely in the control of the Lord Jesus Christ, represents the beginning of the outpouring of God's wrath upon this world. At this point, there is a great deal more of the Tribulation still to run its course. Note the wording of the following verse in Revelation chapter 15:

> *And I saw another sign in heaven, great and marvelous, seven angels having seven plagues, which are the last,* ***for in them is finished the wrath of God.***
> *(Revelation 15:1 RV)*

Clearly, if these seven plagues 'finish' (other translations use 'complete') the wrath of God, then it must have been the wrath of God being executed up until that time. We have still not reached the Second Coming of the Lord Jesus at this point, although it is getting closer. However, this proves that God's wrath includes the whole of the Tribulation period, not just the end of it.

Satan's wrath is mentioned in the following verse:

> *Therefore rejoice, ye heavens, and ye that dwell in them. Woe to the inhabiters of the earth and of the sea! for* ***the devil is come down unto you, having great wrath,*** *because he knoweth that he hath but a short time. (Revelation 12:12)*

A careful study of the context of this verse in Revelation chapter 12 and other related scriptures will show that this happens at the midpoint of the seven year Tribulation. The verse tells us *why* he has great wrath. It is simply because he has only a short time left before his counterfeit kingdom is brought to an end. This gives no justification for declaring that the purpose of the seven year Tribulation period is for the outpouring Satan's wrath. Just as we saw earlier that Israel's Babylonian captivity was primarily the result of God's chastisement upon their continued sin. Doubtless, Nebuchadnezzar may have been wrathful, but this was practically incidental, being eclipsed by the sovereign purposes of Almighty God.

The notion that the *"Day of the Lord"* does not include the Tribulation is further shown to be wrong by the following verses:

> *(1 Thessalonians 5:2) For yourselves know perfectly that* ***the day of the Lord*** *so* ***cometh as a thief in the night.***

> *(1 Thessalonians 5:3) For* ***when they shall say, Peace and safety; then sudden destruction cometh upon them,*** *as travail upon a woman with child; and they shall not escape.*

Here we are given a vital piece of information. The *"Day of the Lord"* will come suddenly, at a time when the world least expects it. At some point, perhaps a little while after the Rapture that Paul had been describing in the previous chapter, the remaining world population could well have begun to recover from their shock and bewilderment. Most will almost certainly have fallen for an official, spurious explanation concerning the missing millions of people. The likely stratagem would appear to have been a long time in the making and is ready to be rolled out even in our present-day. In chapter 6 we will look in more detail at the possible sort of deception that could be used by deceived and deceiving political and religious leaders at that time.

At this point, the Lord Jesus Christ will have opened the first seal (Revelation 6:1-2). Most teachers of Bible prophecy are agreed that the rider on the white horse represents the Antichrist, who will begin his gradual ascendancy to total power with a deceptive false peace. No doubt he and other world leaders will be congratulating themselves and saying *"Peace and Safety"* (1 Thessalonians 5:3). This delusion will be short-lived and shattered by the opening of the second seal which brings war and destruction.

For those who say that the *"Day of the Lord"* does not begin until after the seven year Tribulation period there is a major problem. Can anyone seriously imagine that after seven years of overwhelming devastation throughout the world, people will be declaring, *"Peace and Safety"*? Clearly not. Not only that, but is the supposed entrance of the *"Day of the Lord"*, after this short but shattering time period, really likely to come as a *"Thief in the Night"* to survivors? Again, hardly likely.

6. The Rapture cannot occur until after the 'apostasy' or 'falling away' occurs.

Answer: This claim is based on the following verses:

(2 Thessalonians 2:1-3 RV) Now we beseech you, brethren, touching the coming of our Lord Jesus Christ, and our gathering together unto him;

(2 Thessalonians 2:2) to the end that ye be not quickly shaken from your mind, nor yet be troubled, either by spirit, or by word, or by epistle as from us, as that ***the day of the Lord is now present;***

(2 Thessalonians 2:3) let no man beguile you in any wise: ***for it will not be, except the falling away come first, and the man of sin be revealed, the son of perdition,***

As always, context is all important. In his first letter to the Thessalonians, Paul had given them rich instruction concerning the Rapture and the *"Day of the Lord"* that would follow it. It would appear that, at some point after that first letter, the Thessalonians had fallen prey to some false teaching, purporting to come from Paul himself. It was alleged that the *"Day of the Lord"* had arrived and that they had therefore entered the seven year Tribulation period. At the time, they were enduring severe persecution, which gave the deception a veneer of plausibility.

No wonder they were upset and bewildered and needed a second epistle from Paul to put the matter straight and relieve their anxiety. Originally, they had been clearly taught that the Rapture of the Church had to occur before the *"Day of the Lord"* could commence. Now, as a direct result of heeding false doctrine, they were in distress, thinking that the teaching on the pre-Tribulation Rapture had been wrong and that they were now in the *"Day of the Lord"*.

Paul's concern was to restore their comfort and peace of mind. He did this firstly by exhorting them not to be beguiled or deceived in any way (verse 3). Secondly, he clearly stated the order of major End Time events (verse 3) and thirdly, reminded them that he had clearly taught them these things whilst he was with them (verse 5).

The confusion over the interpretation of this passage is largely caused by the translation of the Greek word *'apostasia'* in verse 3. Most modern translations have followed the lead of the King James Version and translated *'apostasia'* as *"the falling away"*, *"the rebellion"* or similar. Some have simply used the word *"apostasy"*, which is not a translation but rather a transliteration. For any true Christian, the word *"apostasy"* is usually understood to mean a defection from the true Faith. However, is this what Paul had in mind when he used the Greek word *'apostasia'*?

Dr. Thomas Ice has written a very thought-provoking and well-argued article called, *"The Rapture in 2 Thessalonians 2:3"*. In it he notes that the first seven English translations of the Bible prior to the King James Version perfectly correctly translated *'apostasia'* as *"the departure"* or *"departing"*. This has huge implications. He also observes that the word is preceded by the definite article *'the'* in the original. This means that Paul was referring to a definite event known to the Thessalonians and himself. There are clearly major problems with insisting that defection from the Faith had been his meaning. The Scriptures make it clear that apostasy has been around since the earliest days of the Church, so what would constitute *the* apostasy? At no point prior to the verse we are considering had Paul taught the Thessalonians about a future defection from the Faith, let alone a very definite act of such. With that in mind, what were the Thessalonians to make of Paul's sudden mention of defection from the Faith, without any prior foundational instruction or current amplification? Clearly, they would have been bewildered and wondered what on earth Paul meant!

However, there is yet another logical reason why Paul could not have meant a future defection from the Faith. This concerns one of the very reasons that Paul was writing to the Thessalonians for a second time, namely to comfort them and put their minds at rest by reassuring them that the *"Day of the Lord"* had not already commenced, as they had been falsely told. As we have already said, they were expecting to be caught up to meet the Lord Jesus in the air prior to the revealing of the Antichrist and commencement of the *"Day of the Lord"*. Is it really likely they would be comforted by Paul's assurances that they were not in the *"Day of the Lord"* because a wholesale falling away from the Faith had to come first? Would *we* be comforted much by being told such a thing? Conversely, if Paul's meaning had been to re-emphasise that *"the departure"* (i.e. the Rapture) must precede the revealing of the Antichrist (*"man of sin"*) and the *"Day of the Lord"*, these difficulties and contradictions all disappear.

Just a few verses further on in 2 Thessalonians chapter 2 we are given another strong pointer to the logic of a pre-Tribulation Rapture.

> *(2 Thessalonians 2:6) And now ye know what withholdeth* [restrains] *that he* [Antichrist] *might be revealed in his time.*

> *(2 Thessalonians 2:7) For the mystery of iniquity doth already work: only* ***he*** *who now letteth* [restrains] *will let* [restrain], ***until he be taken out of the way.***

(2 Thessalonians 2:8) ***And then shall that Wicked*** [Antichrist] ***be revealed,*** *whom the Lord shall consume with the spirit of his mouth, and shall destroy with the brightness of his coming:*

In these remarkable verses and those that follow, we are taught that there is currently a restraint being exercised, preventing Satan from bringing forth his counterfeit Messiah, the Antichrist. This restrainer is referred to by the personal pronoun *"he"* in verse 7. Whilst there have been many suggestions as to what or who the restrainer could be, there is really only one satisfactory answer. Clearly, the restrainer must be a person in order to be referred to as *"he"*. Further to that, there is only one Person with the power to hold back Satan and that Person is God. Since the Holy Spirit is the member of the Godhead currently on Earth, it is entirely reasonable to believe that He is the restrainer being referred to. In recognition of this, some Bibles (such as the New King James Version) have capitalised the personal pronoun in verse 7, making it *"He"*.

This passage presents us with a logical harmony concerning the sequence of events leading up to the revealing of Antichrist and commencement of the *"Day of the Lord"*. What do we mean? We have already sought to show that 2 Thessalonians 2:3 makes much more sense in the earliest English translations, with renderings such as *"the departure"*, which is a clear reference to the Rapture, rather than *"the falling away"* of more recent versions, which makes little sense in the context. From this we learn that the Antichrist *cannot* be revealed until after *"the departure"* of the true Church. In other words, it is not an enormous act of apostasy that facilitates the appearing of Antichrist, but rather the complete removal of the true Church. This understanding of sequence is very much confirmed by verses 6 to 8. In these we also read that, far from it being a specific act of apostasy that brings the Antichrist into the arena, it is the sudden and complete removal of a hitherto exercised Divine restraint that will allow Satan to bring forth his Antichrist. The logical conclusion from this is that the Holy Spirit will cease His restraint upon evil in this world at the same time as the true Church is removed from Earth to Heaven at the Rapture. Doubtless the Holy Spirit currently exercises some of this restraint through the presence of true Christians in the world. After all, we are supposed to be salt and light, both of which represent a preservative quality and restraint upon surrounding evil. Unquestionably the Holy Spirit is able to exercise restraint upon evil through the true Church or entirely without visible means. However, it would seem to be God's purpose to remove both the true Church and all restraint upon evil simultaneously.

Before moving on, and to prevent any misunderstanding, we need to clarify that the Bible does indeed teach that apostasy (in the sense of departure from the Faith), which has been around since the earliest days of the Church, will become much more widespread and aggravated within the professing church in the last of the Last Days. Passages such as 2 Timothy chapter 3 and chapter 4:1-4, 2 Peter chapters 2 and 3 and the book of Jude leave us in no doubt about that. Therefore the expectation of widespread apostasy within the professing church in the End Times is not dependent upon a very doubtful translation of 2 Thessalonians 2:3 because it is clearly established elsewhere by Paul, Peter and Jude.

This brings us to a most interesting but seldom thought-about point. In the aftermath of the Rapture, it will not be at all obvious to the unbelieving world that it is the Church that has gone. Why not? Simply because there will be vast numbers of professing Christians and church members still on Earth. We need to remember that the Lord Jesus Christ is coming for His Bride, the true Church, which is composed entirely and exclusively of all truly born-again believers. There will be none who are Christian in name only included in the Rapture.

The Roman Catholic Church will almost certainly be the least affected by the Rapture, with only a small proportion of their members missing. Usually when a Catholic person gets saved by coming to know the truth, it is not long before they realise that God's Word teaches that His children should separate from all such false religious systems. The Protestant denominations, now so seriously compromised or even apostate, may well be left with many of their membership still on Earth. The proportion of members missing will no doubt vary from church to church as some are far further down the apostate road than others. I believe it is very likely, tragically, that even so-called 'evangelical' and 'Bible-believing' churches will have those within their ranks left behind after the Rapture because they had never been genuinely born-again.

This will help to make it relatively easy for the world's wicked religious leadership to claim that God's real 'church' is here on Earth. Having been 'cleansed' by the removal of all those 'troublesome, bigoted and intolerant fundamentalists', the real 'church' will now be ready to complete the long cherished merger with all world religions, thus forming the one-world false religion foretold in the Bible. The likely sort of deception that world political and religious authorities will use to explain away the missing millions will be discussed in chapter 6.

CHAPTER 4

DEALING WITH OBJECTIONS (PART 2)

7. The Secret Rapture doctrine is not found anywhere in the Bible.

Answer: This is somewhat similar to the first objection we looked at, which was the claim that the word 'Rapture' does not appear in the Bible. However, the emphasis this time is upon the word 'Secret'. The use of the phrase "Secret Rapture" seems to be an attempt to portray the doctrine of the pre-Tribulation Rapture as novel or even ridiculous. The great irony with this is that I have yet to hear anyone who faithfully teaches the pre-Tribulation Rapture describe it as the "Secret Rapture"!

Nevertheless, in the interest of fairness, we need to examine precisely what the Scriptures teach on the matter to determine whether or not any aspect of the event we call the Rapture could be described as secret. Before we do that though, let us take a brief look at the 'bigger picture' of why so many outside, as well as inside, the Church remain so woefully unaware of soon-coming events.

Governments, Security Services and Armed Forces all possess, as well as originate, secret documents that are kept very securely so that only authorised persons can view them. In complete contrast, God has made known in the New Testament His intention to catch away the true Church to Heaven. The New Testament has existed for nearly twenty centuries! It has also become freely available to many in the world in their own language, thus the fact that there is going to be a Rapture could hardly be described as a secret. Granted, many do not know about it, either because they profess no faith in Christ or are only nominal Christians. Even true Christians can be in ignorance due to lack of Bible knowledge or subscribing to a faulty theological system. For example, Amillennialism, which fails to interpret the prophetic Scriptures literally, as they were intended to be read. How tragic that, unless awakened by God's grace, unsaved people (including many who profess to be Christian) adopt an attitude of willing ignorance to God's Word and especially to those parts dealing with mankind's true history (Creation, Fall, Noah's Flood etc.) and those dealing with future events (End Time prophecies). How sadly ironic that such folk little realise that they are actually fulfilling one of many prophecies that describe our day.

> *For this they **willingly** are **ignorant** of, that by the word of God the heavens were of old, and the earth standing out of the water and in the water:* (2 Peter 3:5)

We would encourage you to read the whole of chapter 3 from which this verse is taken. Speaking prophetically, the Holy Spirit tells us through Peter what will be the characteristic attitude of so many as we near the Second Coming of the Lord Jesus Christ. It is highly significant that the scoffers *wilfully choose* to remain ignorant of Earth's true history which, in turn, leads to a mocking attitude and obliviousness concerning the certainty of coming judgement. However, widespread ignorance concerning the Rapture is not at all the same thing as it being a secret.

Having said all this and in the interest of even-handedness, many who use the phrase, "Secret Rapture", do not so much have in mind the whole event, but rather certain specifics concerning *how* it will occur. It can be clearly deduced from relevant passages that the world in general will not see Jesus when He comes to collect His Bride, the true Church. But why should this present such a difficulty? Did He show Himself to all and sundry after His resurrection? Clearly not. In His resurrection body, He only revealed Himself to those who had believed on Him and in the case of Paul, as part of his dramatic conversion on the road to Damascus. The Scriptures make it clear that at the Rapture, the Lord Jesus Christ will catch up His waiting Church to meet Him in the air and specifically in the clouds. It is not God's purpose or intention to reveal the Lord Jesus to the world in general at this point; that comes later.

> *Then we which are alive and remain shall be caught up together with them* ***in the clouds,*** *to meet the Lord* ***in the air:*** *and so shall we ever be with the Lord.*
> *(1 Thessalonians 4:17)*

This verse is taken from the classic Rapture passage, 1 Thessalonians 4:13-18. It is vital to understand that this is not describing the Lord Jesus Christ's Second Advent in glory, when he will descend all the way to Earth in judgement to set up His Kingdom for 1000 years on Earth. The first allusion to the Rapture is given by the Lord Jesus Himself in the following passage:

> *(John 14:1) Let not your heart be troubled: ye believe in God, believe also in me.*

> *(John 14:2) In my Father's house are many mansions: if it were not so, I would have told you.* ***I go to prepare a place for you.***

> *(John 14:3) And if I go and prepare a place for you,* ***I will come again, and receive you unto myself; that where I am, there ye may be also.***

Whilst God deferred a full revelation of the doctrine of the Rapture until it was given to the apostle Paul, we are nonetheless given a tantalising glimpse of its purpose in these words of the Lord Jesus. In terms of who is going where and for what purpose, the above passage is unambiguous. It makes clear that, in His absence and among many other things, Jesus is preparing a place in Heaven for us. He will then come again for the express purpose of receiving us unto Himself and taking us to the completed place in Heaven that He has prepared.

This clearly has nothing whatsoever to do with His Second Advent in glory when He will descend all the way to Earth in the sight of the whole world. His purpose will be to save the surviving remnant of Israel from destruction at the hands of the Antichrist and the world's armies and then to set up His Kingdom. The Antichrist and False Prophet will be captured and hurled alive into the lake of fire. All that have followed them will be killed by the Word of the Lord at this point. It is interesting to note from Revelation chapter 19 that the Lord Jesus Christ is accompanied by His Bride, the true Church, as He leaves Heaven and descends to Earth. Clearly, from simple logic, the completed Church must have previously been caught up to Heaven to be able to accompany her Heavenly Bridegroom as He descends to Earth to reign. A straightforward understanding that the Rapture must occur at least seven years before this point (and therefore before the Tribulation period) fits all of the relevant Scriptures perfectly. Confusing these two entirely different events leads to making an illogical muddle of the prophetic Scriptures.

Returning to the objection to a *secret* Rapture, it should be noted that none of the Scriptures referring to the Rapture either use the word 'secret' or even imply that secrecy is the main feature of the event. The fact that the world will not see Jesus when the Rapture takes place is simply because it does not concern them; Jesus is coming exclusively for His own and the unbelieving world has no part or place in the matter. We saw from 1 Thessalonians 4:17 that the rendezvous of believers with the Lord Jesus will take place in the air and specifically in *the clouds.* At His Ascension, we are told that a cloud received Jesus out of the sight of the disciples.

> *And when he had spoken these things, while they beheld, he was taken up; and* ***a cloud received him out of their sight.*** *(Acts 1:9)*

It seems entirely consistent that clouds will also prevent a Christ-rejecting world from observing this awesomely holy and intimate moment as His Bride is caught up into her Heavenly Bridegroom's immediate presence.

> *Which also said, Ye men of Galilee, why stand ye gazing up into heaven? this same Jesus, which is taken up from you into heaven,* ***shall so come in like manner*** *as ye have seen him go into heaven. (Acts 1:11)*

It is sobering that it is not God's intention that those who have decidedly rejected Him should understand what has happened at the Rapture. Indeed, just a little while later He will send those who have had no love of the truth a *powerful delusion.*

> *(2 Thessalonians 2:10b) …* ***they received not the love of the truth,*** *that they might be saved.*

> *(2 Thessalonians 2:11) And for this cause* ***God shall send them strong delusion,*** *that they should believe a lie:*

It has been conjectured that the geographical place of rendezvous at the Rapture will be high above the city of

Jerusalem. Whilst this is entirely possible, if not probable, we cannot be dogmatic on such a point because the Scriptures do not tell us. However, one speaker cited his belief that the whole event would be seen on Israeli air defence radars as one of his reasons for dismissing it! I will not comment further on that assertion, but let you the reader decide on the credibility of such an objection.

In conclusion, it tends to be only those who dismiss the pre-Tribulation Rapture that refer to it as 'secret'. This tends to portray the doctrine as fantastical and therefore ridiculous. A straightforward reading and comparison of the Scriptures indicates that the Rapture will most definitely happen and that it must occur before the beginning of the Tribulation, whether men like it or not. Why some Christians kick and fight against this must be a matter between them and the Lord.

8. The timing of the Rapture is only a secondary doctrine and therefore not really important.

Answer: There is a lovely parallel between the way a typical Jewish wedding would have been conducted whilst Jesus was on Earth and the sequence of events at and after the Rapture. This can be obscured by our Western notion of a wedding, which is very different to the ancient Jewish pattern. The major difference that concerns us is that in the Jewish pattern the bridegroom comes to collect the bride from her home, whereas in the Western tradition the bride is brought to the bridegroom at the place where the wedding ceremony will happen.

We shall only concern ourselves with the Jewish pattern. The couple who are to be married would already be betrothed to each other: an arrangement much more binding than a typical Western engagement. In the normal course of events, the bride would be longing for the day when the bridegroom would arrive to take her from her parents' home, though she did not know precisely what time he would arrive. What could be said of the bride's attitude towards and 'love' for her bridegroom if she was indifferent to his coming and, perhaps secretly, did not want him to come too soon? Perhaps she occupied herself with other matters rather than making sure she was ready for his arrival, convincing herself that many other things had to happen first before he could be expected to make an appearance. Such a bride would show herself to be thoroughly unworthy of her bridegroom and to have little love for him.

Is it not alarmingly easy to draw a parallel between this depressing scenario and the all too common attitude to the Rapture to be found amongst so many in today's 'Bible-believing' churches? Can we really deny that such attitudes are a reliable gauge of the Laodicean lukewarmness that characterises so much of the professing church in these Last Days? "But our pastor doesn't teach on End Times and doesn't believe in a pre-Tribulation Rapture" protests someone. However, is there anywhere in the Word of God that limits us to the ministry of one man? We have His Word in our own language. There is also a wealth of good teaching material available in books, on CDs, DVDs and the Internet. Whilst we need to exercise caution and spiritual discernment with these sources of instruction, due to the existence of much misleading and false doctrine, this should not stop us from learning to feed ourselves. God expects us to grow up into mature disciples rather than remaining as spiritual babes.

Let us turn again to the Scriptures and ask ourselves

another searching question. In the many places where the apostle Paul wrote concerning the Rapture and/or the Second Coming, did he ever give even a hint that the matter was 'secondary' and that various irreconcilable views on the subject were quite acceptable and even to be expected? On the contrary, he went out of his way to emphasise the importance of the issue and, when necessary, to correct false teaching on the matter. Take the following verses that we looked at previously in answering objection number 6:

(2 Thessalonians 2:1-3 RV) ***Now we beseech you,*** *brethren, touching the coming of our Lord Jesus Christ, and our gathering together unto him;*

(2 Thessalonians 2:2) ***to the end that ye be not quickly shaken from your mind, nor yet be troubled,*** *either by spirit, or by word, or by epistle as from us, as that the day of the Lord is now present;*

(2 Thessalonians 2:3) ***let no man beguile you in any wise:*** *for it will not be, except the falling away* come first, and the man of sin be revealed, the son of perdition,*

(*See answer to objection number 6 for an explanation of the problem with the translation rendered, *"the falling away"*)

In these verses it is particularly clear, from the emboldened words, that Paul is using emphatic and explicit language to ensure a correct understanding of a vital doctrine. He does not say that since the matter is not a 'salvation issue' it is not really all that important. If the order of End Time events was really a matter of such little consequence, why would Paul exhort the Thessalonian believers not to be beguiled (i.e. deceived) by false teachers?

Let us ask another penetrating question: If God

considered it vital that the believers of Paul's generation had a clear understanding of the relationship of the Rapture to End Time events, is it really conceivable that He thinks it much less of an issue for today's believers who are so much closer to this wondrous event? Clearly, God knew that the Rapture would not take place in Paul's day. Someone will ask, "Why then was it important for the Thessalonian believers to understand that the Rapture must occur before the Day of the Lord?" The answer is simple and vitally important. False teaching had alarmed them by insinuating that the Day of the Lord (i.e. the Tribulation) had already begun. This had a measure of plausibility to them because they were already suffering persecution. However, a firm understanding that the Rapture *must* occur before the Tribulation would have been a comfort to them and enabled them to dismiss the teaching as false. It is clear from Paul's writings that he considered the Rapture to be a distinct possibility in his day. We know this from the following passages:

> *(1 Corinthians 15:51) Behold, I shew you a mystery;* ***We*** *shall not all sleep, but* ***we*** *shall all be changed,*
>
> *(1 Corinthians 15:52) In a moment, in the twinkling of an eye, at the last trump: for the trumpet shall sound, and the dead shall be raised incorruptible, and* ***we*** *shall be changed.*
>
> *(1 Thessalonians 4:13) But I would not have you to be ignorant, brethren, concerning them which are asleep, that ye sorrow not, even as others which have no hope.*
>
> *(1 Thessalonians 4:14) For if we believe that Jesus died and rose again, even so them also which sleep in Jesus will God bring with him.*
>
> *(1 Thessalonians 4:15) For this we say unto you by the word*

of the Lord, that **we** *which are alive and remain unto the coming of the Lord shall not prevent them which are asleep.*

(1 Thessalonians 4:16) *For the Lord himself shall descend from heaven with a shout, with the voice of the archangel, and with the trump of God: and the dead in Christ shall rise first:*

(1 Thessalonians 4:17) *Then* **we** *which are alive and remain shall be caught up together with them in the clouds, to meet the Lord in the air: and so shall* **we** *ever be with the Lord.*

(1 Thessalonians 4:18) *Wherefore comfort one another with these words.*

Notice Paul's continuous use of the personal pronoun *we* rather than *you*, which makes it abundantly clear that he believed that he could take part in an imminent Rapture. Does the fact that Paul was eventually put to death invalidate his prior expectation of being caught up to meet the Lord in the air? Not at all! God alone knows the date of the Rapture but can nonetheless legitimately hold it out as an imminent and comforting expectation to every generation of true Christians. He can do this because He has promised that it will occur *before* the Tribulation period, no matter how long it be delayed.

All of this has a tremendous significance for the present day. Amongst too many believers who have at least *some* understanding that we are close to the end of this present Age there is, regrettably, enormous confusion in their understanding of Bible prophecy. In a similar way that the Thessalonian believers were troubled by a false teaching claiming that they were already in the Day of the Lord, we have today a proliferation of those who would try to convince us that the Church will go through some or all of the Tribulation. If they were correct, simple logic would lead to the conclusion that the Rapture cannot be imminent or, in other words, could not happen *today, tomorrow, next week or even next year.* This has grave implications for all Christian believers. It means that, if we do not enter the Lord's presence through death in the meantime, we are all headed for a soon-coming period of unparalleled horror upon the Earth as God pours out His wrath on a Christ-rejecting world. The descriptions of this period in the Hebrew Scriptures (Old Testament), Gospels and book of Revelation can leave no doubt that it will be a time of unprecedented terror as progressive supernatural judgements rain down upon sinful mankind. The majority of those who turn to Christ and refuse to worship the Antichrist will be martyred by beheading.

Can this scenario in which the Rapture features part way through or at the end of the Tribulation really be described as a *"blessed hope"?* For any Christian facing up to the terrifying reality of the Tribulation, it can only produce a sense of dark foreboding. In an attempt to address this obvious dilemma, some prophecy teachers say things like, "Don't worry, God's grace will enable you to bear it", or equivalent. However, let us consider the ways of God. When He deals with us as individuals, He does not inform us in advance about particular trials or personal tragedies that might be a part of the path mapped out for us. This is because in His love for us, He does not want us troubled by such a foreknowledge of the future for which He will provide the needed grace at the time. Does it really seem likely that He would set before us the Tribulation period (a period far worse than anything likely to be encountered in the life of most believers) and expect us to be comforted that the Rapture is to occur partway through or at the end of it? I have no hesitation in totally rejecting such a notion and I pray, dear reader, that you will too.

Let us remind ourselves that we are answering the objection that the Rapture is only a so-called 'secondary doctrine' and therefore its timing is 'not really important'. Surely, the more one stops and thinks about the awesome and stupendous nature of the event that we call the Rapture, the more preposterous it becomes to believe that it is a matter of only secondary importance. It is nothing less than the Lord Jesus Christ, the Heavenly Bridegroom, descending into Earth's atmosphere to collect His Bride, the true Church, made up of every truly born-again man, woman and child, dead and living, from the day of His resurrection until that point. He will then take her to the place that He has prepared for her in Heaven. Does that sound secondary?

A further thought comes to mind when one considers the way of thinking behind the modern ecumenical movement. Compromised churches are willing to water down or even abandon the vital, foundational doctrine of salvation itself in order to unite with each other and, ultimately, with the Church of Rome. The 'unity' produced is, of course, man-made and not of God. It is highly significant that one rarely, if ever, finds Christians who have a love of the Word of God and a measure of understanding of Bible prophecy involved in any way with the ecumenical movement. The reason for this is simply that they are able to discern that the spirit behind the ecumenical movement is not the Holy Spirit because of the compromise and departure from the Word of God involved. Is it not then an irony that amongst many Bible prophecy teachers there seems to be an almost unspoken rule that one must not be dogmatic concerning the timing of the Rapture? With the best of intentions (i.e.

to avoid arguments and discord), totally irreconcilable views are deemed to be acceptable. This seems unwittingly to adopt the same principles as the ecumenical movement, albeit not over the matter of salvation itself. Again, we need to remind ourselves that the Rapture is no trifling matter, but represents the hope to which every well-instructed Christian should be looking.

It is clear from what the Scriptures reveal about the nature of Satan that he desires to have the pre-eminence that belongs to God alone. He already has unbelieving mankind dancing to his tune and embracing his ways. He wants man's attention focused on his works and not God's. Many of today's politicians are so clearly animated by the spirit of antichrist, as evidenced by the increase in godless and God-defying legislation they produce. Godless policies are embraced by godless people, therefore it is not difficult to see how readily the masses will embrace Satan's counterfeit 'messiah', the Antichrist, when God initiates his revelation after the Rapture. But Satan is not satisfied with the attention of unbelievers alone. Sadly, he has had great success in turning the attention of many Christians more upon the coming Antichrist than the even sooner coming Christ! How has this been achieved? Clearly, a pre-Tribulation Rapture is the *only* doctrine that would keep the eyes of Christians looking expectantly for the imminent appearing of the Lord Jesus Christ. Every doctrine that places the Rapture either in or at the end of the Tribulation period must logically cause Christians to be looking for the Antichrist, whether knowingly or not. Absolutely nowhere in Scripture are we told to be looking for the Antichrist but, on the contrary, we are exhorted time and again to be looking for the Lord Jesus Christ's appearing for us in verses such as the following:

> ***Looking for*** *that blessed hope, and* ***the glorious appearing of the great God and our Saviour Jesus Christ;*** *(Titus 2:13)*

> ***And to wait for his Son from heaven,*** *whom he raised from the dead,* ***even Jesus, which delivered*** [who delivers] ***us from the wrath to come.*** *(1 Thessalonians 1:10)*

> *For our conversation is in heaven; from whence also* ***we look for the Saviour, the Lord Jesus Christ:*** *(Philippians 3:20)*

> *So that ye come behind in no gift;* ***waiting for the coming of our Lord Jesus Christ:*** *(1 Corinthians 1:7)*

Let us not give heed to those who would twist the clear meaning out of these verses and many others like them, but rather embrace the truth and rejoice in the comfort that God intends for His Church! Clearly, anyone who embraces the truth of a pre-Tribulation Rapture should not be duped by Satan into having their attention totally absorbed with events down here on Earth and consequently looking for the appearance of Antichrist. It is for this reason, as well as the strength and courage that such a hope produces in trials and afflictions, that Satan clearly hates the teaching of a pre-Tribulation Rapture. This would explain the un-Christ-like behaviour of some within the Church as they attack not just the doctrine of a pre-Tribulation Rapture itself, but also those who teach it.

An interesting inconsistency is that, so often, those who say that the Rapture timing is not a major issue, then go out of their way to try and prove that the Church must go through the Tribulation period! Why do this if the matter is of so little importance? Similarly, those who hold to differing Rapture timings *within* the seven year Tribulation period (such as the 'Mid' and 'Post' Tribulation positions) rarely take issue with each other's teaching, but rather tend to unite against the position perceived as the 'common enemy', namely the pre-Tribulation Rapture. Can this be a coincidence?

A further thought occurs concerning sick or elderly saints who might not realistically be expected to live for very much longer. Are they to be excluded from the *"blessed hope"* because the Rapture is supposedly always at least 3½ years away if the Antichrist has not yet been revealed? One might answer that the *"dead in Christ shall rise first"* according to 1 Thessalonians 4:16. Whilst this is blessedly true, the proper hope of a Christian is not death, but rather to be among the living whom the Lord will catch up to meet Him in the air at the Rapture. One preacher put it well when he said that we should be looking for the 'upper-taker' not the undertaker!

> *For we that are in this tabernacle* [body] *do groan, being burdened:* ***not for that we would be unclothed, but clothed upon,*** *that mortality might be swallowed up of life. (2 Corinthians 5:4)*

In the passage from which the above verse is taken, Paul speaks of the present mortal body of a believer as a tabernacle or tent that will be taken down at the point of physical death, leaving the saved soul in a dis-embodied or 'naked' state awaiting the future, physical resurrection of the body. However, he teaches that rather than that being the main focus of our hope, we should be looking for and hoping to be among those Christians who will not experience physical death but rather be *"clothed upon"* with immortality, thereby having our mortal bodies transformed into a resurrection body in an instant. Does it seem likely that God would expect Christians nearing the end of their earthly lives to abandon this particular hope and prospect? Further to this, if the Church was really destined to go through the Tribulation, the vast majority would be martyred, rendering Paul's teaching on the proper hope of a Christian irrelevant to the greater part of the End Time Church.

In conclusion, one's belief about the timing of the Rapture has major consequences in terms of one's whole prophetic outlook and expectation. Confusion and conflicting views over the issue are most certainly not the necessary and inevitable state of the Church in these closing days of the present Age. The truth needs to be taught graciously but fearlessly and without regard to the oppositions of men.

9. The Church needs to go through the Tribulation in order to be purified.

Answer: Some commentators have described this assertion as "Contending for a Protestant version of Purgatory". One can understand why. Probably unintentionally, such a claim strikes at the very heart of Christ's finished work on the cross. It surely cannot be a coincidence that the majority of those who teach this sort of thing also teach that a true Christian can lose their salvation. I do not hesitate to say that I believe this to be a very serious false doctrine, which one hears taught, either directly or indirectly, with alarming frequency. The faulty theology or 'leaven' behind both doctrines is essentially the same and fails to fully understand the marvel of God's salvation, bestowed by His free grace upon undeserving sinners. What Christ declared on the cross to be "finished", they have effectively, if unintentionally, declared to be 'almost finished'. The most serious effect of this is to rob God of the glory due to His Name that flows from a finished redemption. Next in order of damage done is the fear instilled into the hearts of God's people who give heed to such teachings. One cannot reach any level of maturity as a disciple of the Lord Jesus Christ without having faced many divinely appointed trials, designed to teach us the futility of looking to our own strength to maintain ourselves in the walk of faith. C H Spurgeon wisely pointed out that if only the last stitch in the garment of salvation was left for us to insert, then we would be for ever undone.

It is not within the scope of this book to enter into a full defence of the precious doctrine of the eternal security of the believer. That has been done very ably and many times over by other teachers and writers. Suffice to say that salvation is of God *alone* and that man can no more maintain himself in a state of grace than he can procure salvation in the first place by his own efforts. It seems to be a hidden, works-based leaven that lies at the root of both denying eternal security and insisting that the Church *needs* to go through the Tribulation. One of the most curious and baffling phenomena one encounters in connection with these things is the attitude of some Christians to them. The thought that they could lose their salvation and end up in the Lake of Fire seems to be precious to them and, in some cases, they refuse to hear any scriptural challenge to their position. Similarly, they seem to relish the notion that they have the Tribulation period just ahead of them and disdain to have the scriptural inconsistency of such a position pointed out to them. This is mysterious indeed and can only be adequately explained by realising that there must be a deep-seated leaven at work.

Another factor is that some well-meaning Bible teachers and preachers appear to be afraid of God's grace, mistakenly believing that it gives a licence to sin. Doubtless the cheap 'grace' advanced by some of today's false teachers does indeed give a licence to continue in a life of sin after supposedly being 'converted'. However, we should not allow the existence of the false to cause us to doubt the reality of the God-glorifying marvel of true grace. True grace does not produce a desire to continue in a life of sin as though it did not matter. On the contrary, the new nature imparted, when the Holy Spirit regenerates us, hates sin and desires to live entirely for the glory of God, constantly warring against the old sin nature.

It can sometimes be helpful to our understanding of these sorts of issues to ask some simple questions. For example, to those who claim that the Church *needs* to go through the Tribulation, we could ask the following question: "Considering the fact that a huge proportion of the Church is *already* in Heaven, chosen of God the Father, saved by the blood of the Lamb and sanctification of the Holy Spirit, why do you insist that the End Time Church requires the additional 'purification' of passing through the Tribulation?". Clearly, there is no reasonable answer that can be given to this. Here is another question: "Most of us know some fellow believers who have already gone home to Glory and perhaps some quite recently. If the Tribulation was to start this year, would these believers need to be specially resurrected in order to join with us who are still alive, so that they too might be 'purified' enough by enduring the Tribulation?" Clearly, this is a ludicrous scenario. Nevertheless, we ask these questions in order to expose the biblical inconsistency that lies behind these kinds of teaching.

In conclusion, the Church most certainly does not *need* to go through the Tribulation, which is yet another reason why she will not do so.

10. The doctrine of imminence is disproved by the Lord's foretelling of specific events that were in the near future for certain individuals during the first century.

Answer: This is a recognition that the vital matter of imminence is at the very heart of the whole matter. Imminence means that the Lord Jesus Christ could return for His Church at any moment without any intervening, prophesied events needing to happen first. For this reason some have sought to cast doubt upon imminence by using very flimsy arguments, as we shall see.

We shall look at two examples in this class of objection, which are typical of any further such cases that might be put forward.

Example 1

The Lord Jesus foretold the coming of the Holy Spirit upon the disciples. In order for this prophecy to come to pass, the Rapture could not possibly have happened as they waited for the fulfilment of Jesus' words. If it had happened, the prophetic words of the Lord Jesus would have been proven false. Therefore the Rapture cannot be imminent.

Rebuttal: Perhaps the first thing to point out is that the doctrine of the Rapture was still a 'mystery' at the time Jesus spoke of the coming of the Holy Spirit to the disciples. A 'mystery' in the biblical sense is something that has not previously been clearly revealed in the Scriptures. Although the Lord Jesus briefly alluded to the Rapture in John 14:1-3, He did not give sufficient detail for the disciples to be able to clearly understand that this was a quite separate and distinct event from His Second Advent in glory. It was left to the apostle Paul to reveal the mystery clearly.

(1 Corinthians 15:51) Behold, ***I shew you a mystery;*** *We shall not all sleep, but we shall all be changed,*

(1 Corinthians 15:52) In a moment, in the twinkling of an eye, at the last trump: for the trumpet shall sound, and the dead shall be raised incorruptible, and we shall be changed.

This revelation, along with the further details of the Rapture in 1Thessalonians 4:13-18, was not given to the Church until many years after Jesus had foretold the coming of the Holy Spirit. Obviously God has always known precisely when the Rapture will happen and, at the time of writing, it has still not occurred. Clearly, since the doctrine of an imminent Rapture was not even revealed until many years after the Holy Spirit had come upon the disciples at Pentecost, they would not have even been aware of it, much less expectant of its possible occurrence. It seems almost superfluous to say that God knew full well that He would not initiate the Rapture prior to sending the Holy Spirit upon the disciples, thus rendering His Son a false prophet!

Those who employ these sort of objections often make much of the dictionary definition of the word 'imminent'. It is typically defined as meaning 'impending' or 'about to happen'. However, a further refinement is needed in order to understand what is meant by the biblical doctrine of imminence. The imminence of the Rapture implies not only that it is impending, but also that no other prophesied event *has to happen* beforehand. It is this aspect of imminence that is seized upon in seeking to disprove the pre-Tribulation Rapture by the use of such tenuous arguments.

In dealing with objection number 8, we have already commented on how God can legitimately hold out the prospect of an imminent Rapture to successive generations of Christians whilst all the time knowing that it would not occur in their particular generation. This is only possible if the Church is to be removed from Earth *before* any of the seven year Tribulation period. Why is this? Simply because the Tribulation period begins with a very definite fulfilment of prophecy, namely the revealing of the Antichrist. After that there are many very definite prophesied events to occur throughout the Tribulation period. It is straightforward logic to realise that if the Church was destined to go through the Tribulation, then she would be instructed to be looking for the Antichrist and subsequent events to occur before there was any possibility of the Rapture. Looking for the Lord Jesus before the Tribulation would thus be absolutely futile if this scenario was true. However, we are *never* instructed in the Scriptures to be looking for the Antichrist, and with good reason. Instead, we are exhorted time and time again to be looking for and waiting expectantly for the appearance of the Lord Jesus Christ.

Clearly, the prophesied matters that have a bearing upon the biblical doctrine of imminence, are End Time in nature, that is, relating to the revelation of Antichrist and subsequent events from which the true Church is to be spared. Is it really justifiable or reasonable to take a handful of instances relating solely to individuals in the very early, formative years of the Church's existence and seek to use these to overthrow the many clear and unambiguous statements of Scripture which point unerringly to a pre-Tribulation Rapture?

Example 2

In Acts 23:11, the Lord Jesus appeared to Paul to encourage him. He assured him that just as he had testified of Him in Jerusalem, so he must also testify in Rome. Clearly, if this was to come to pass, there could be no Rapture before Paul arrived in Rome, otherwise the assurance would prove false.

Rebuttal: The reader will readily perceive that this example falls into the same class as the previous one. Perhaps the only difference is that, in this instance, it could be argued that the apostle Paul had begun to teach about the Rapture. He revealed it to the Thessalonians in AD 54 and to the Corinthians in AD 59. The time of the Lord Jesus appearing to Paul in Acts 23:11 was about AD 60.

Again, we are faced here with an objection to 'imminence' based upon a word from the Lord to an individual in the first century concerning a short period of time. Is it reasonable on the basis of this to conclude that the Rapture cannot be imminent throughout all the succeeding centuries of church history and that the Church must therefore go through the Tribulation? I am sure that most would conclude that it is unreasonable. It seems to give the appearance of desperation in trying to disprove 'imminence' in the face of so much scriptural evidence to the contrary. We must again emphasise that the imminence of the Rapture is particularly and necessarily with respect to End Time prophecies. Clearly, all events in world history are under the providential control of God, who knows the end from the beginning; God's Word does not contradict itself when 'rightly divided'.

CHAPTER 5

TYPES AND SHADOWS

After the necessary task of dealing with the various attacks made upon our 'Blessed Hope' in the last chapter, it is refreshing to be able to turn our attention to the uplifting study of 'types and shadows' in the Hebrew Scriptures (Old Testament).

For the purpose of this book we shall not embark upon an extensive study of this fascinating and rewarding aspect of the Hebrew Scriptures, but confine ourselves to those types and shadows relevant to the pre-Tribulation Rapture. What are types and shadows? They are basically persons, events, objects, rituals or a combination of any of these that bear a striking similarity to a Person (God the Father, the Lord Jesus Christ or the Holy Spirit) and/or events or series of events that are clearly revealed in the New Testament. It is important to point out that, whilst we do not take our doctrine from types and shadows, we are most certainly expected to look for them having clearly established right doctrine from the New Testament. In 1 Corinthians 10:1-11, Paul teaches that the literal history of God's dealings with Israel foreshadows vital spiritual truths that he was writing about. In this sense types and shadows can be regarded as confirming rather than establishing doctrine.

> *Now these things happened unto them* ***by way of example****; and they were* ***written for our admonition****, upon whom the ends of the ages are come.*
> *(1 Corinthians 10:11 RV)*

In this chapter we shall look at just three types that the reader will readily perceive are a wonderful and powerful confirmation of the pattern of a pre-Tribulation Rapture. It is hoped that these will encourage the reader to search out more of such types and shadows, because the Hebrew Scriptures are a rich mine of them!

I am indebted to the late Clarence Larkin and his extensive work on "Dispensational Truth", from which I have reproduced the numbered points he listed under each type. The first example we shall examine is a thrilling one and it is that of Joseph in the book of Genesis.

JOSEPH A TYPE OF CHRIST

1. *Joseph was "beloved" of his father, so was Jesus.*
2. *Joseph was sent unto his brethren, so was Jesus.*
3. *Joseph's brethren refused to receive him, so did the brethren of Jesus.*
4. *Joseph was sold by his brethren, so was Jesus.*
5. *Joseph was unjustly accused and condemned, so was Jesus.*
6. *Joseph was buried in prison, so was Jesus in the Tomb of Joseph.*
7. *Joseph was resurrected from prison and exalted to sit with Pharaoh on his throne, so Jesus was resurrected and exalted to sit on His Father's Throne.*
8. *Joseph on the throne became the dispenser of bread to starving Egypt, so Jesus on His Father's Throne is the "Bread of Life" for a perishing world.*

9. *After Joseph was exalted he got a Gentile bride, so Jesus will get a Gentile Bride -* **THE CHURCH.**

10. *After Joseph got his bride his brethren suffered famine and came to him for corn, so after Jesus gets His Bride, His brethren, the Jews, will turn to Him, during the time of "Jacob's Trouble", the "Great Tribulation", for relief.*

11. *Joseph knew his brethren the first time, but they did not know him so Jesus knew His brethren when He came the first time but they knew Him not.*

12. *Joseph made himself known to his brethren when they came the "Second time", so Jesus will be recognised by the Jews when He comes the* **SECOND TIME.**

13. *After Joseph's revelation of himself to his brethren, they go forth to proclaim that he is alive and the "saviour of the world", so when Jesus reveals Himself to His brethren the Jews they will proclaim Him alive and the* **SAVIOUR OF MANKIND.**

14. *Joseph then establishes his brethren and their families in the "land of Goshen", so Jesus will re-establish the Jews in the* **LAND OF PALESTINE.** [This should read 'Israel'. The name 'Palestine' should not be used as there was no such place in biblical times and there will be no such place after Jesus returns. Ed.]

From all these wonderful parallels between the life of Joseph and the Lord Jesus, numbers 9 and 10 are the ones that particularly concern us. To these we can add some extra, very interesting details given to us in Genesis chapter 41. In verse 50 we are told the following:

And unto Joseph were born two sons ***before the years of famine came****, which Asenath the daughter of Potipherah priest of On bare unto him.* (Genesis 41:50)

This makes it clear that Joseph's marriage to a Gentile bride was consummated *before* the years of famine came. In like manner, Jesus will consummate His marriage to the Church in the place that He has been preparing for us in Heaven, *before* the Tribulation begins. We know that the Tribulation period will be seven years long. How long was the famine in Joseph's time?

And the ***seven years of dearth*** *began to come, according as Joseph had said: and the dearth was in all lands; but in all the land of Egypt there was bread.* (Genesis 41:54)

Again we see a very precise parallel in the time period of seven years. All these parallels have been placed deliberately in God's Word and are obviously no coincidence. In addition to this, can it be an accident that there are *no* types and shadows that illustrate any of the alternative Rapture timing patterns proposed?

The second example concerns Abraham's servant Eliezer. This is truly moving and surely cannot fail to bring joy to those hungering after truth and righteousness.

ELIEZER A TYPE OF THE HOLY SPIRIT

1. *As Eliezer was a servant of Abraham, so the Holy Spirit is a "****Servant of God****."*

2. *As Eliezer's mission was to go to Haran and get a* ***bride for Isaac****, so the Holy Spirit has been sent from Heaven to get a* ***BRIDE FOR CHRIST****.*

3. *As Eliezer was not sent to get a bride for Isaac until* ***after he was typically offered up****, so the Holy Spirit was not sent to get a Bride for Christ until* ***AFTER HIS DEATH AND RESURRECTION****.*

4. *As Eliezer did not talk* ***about himself, but about his Master's son****, so the Holy Spirit does not talk about* ***HIMSELF, BUT ABOUT CHRIST****.*

5. *As Eliezer was* ***urgent****, so the Holy Spirit is* ***URGENT****, Genesis 24:53-56, 2 Corinthians 6:2*

6. *As Eliezer by the precious gifts he gave Rebekah revealed the wealth of his Master Isaac, so the Holy Spirit by His Gifts gives us a foretaste of what is in store for the Bride of Christ, the Church.*

7. *When Eliezer got Rebekah's consent to be the bride of Isaac* ***he himself took her back;*** *he did not send her back while he remained with her kinsfolk. So when the Bride, the Church, is ready the* ***HOLY SPIRIT WILL GO BACK TO HEAVEN WITH HER****.*

In this wonderful type, all of the parallels are delightful. However, it is number 7 that is of particular interest to us. In dealing with objection number 6 in chapter 3, we looked at a noteworthy aspect of the pre-Tribulation Rapture that involved the Holy Spirit. As we considered 2 Thessalonians chapter 2, we concluded that the restraint, currently being exercised by the Holy Spirit upon lawlessness, will be removed simultaneously with the Rapture of all true Christians.

It is not hard to see these events in Rebekah's life as being analogous to the gathering and subsequent Rapture of the true Church. Rebekah is first of all sought out by Eliezer and then taken by him to be united to Isaac. A further lovely detail that we should not miss is revealed in the chapter from which all these events are taken.

> (Genesis 24:63) ***And Isaac went out*** *to meditate in the field at the eventide: and he lifted up his eyes, and saw, and, behold, the camels were coming.*

> (Genesis 24:64) *And* ***Rebekah lifted up her eyes****, and when* ***she saw Isaac****, she lighted off the camel.*

> (Genesis 24:65) *For she had said unto the servant,* ***What man is this that walketh in the field to meet us?*** *And the servant had said, It is my master: therefore she took a vail, and covered herself.*

Here we see that divine providence had led Isaac out from his dwelling place and into the field to meet his bride. Thus the meeting took place neither at Isaac's tent nor in Rebekah's home country. In like manner, the Lord Jesus will descend from Heaven into Earth's atmosphere (not all the way to Earth, our current dwelling place) and we shall be caught up to meet Him in the air, hallelujah!

> (Genesis 24:66) *And the servant told Isaac all things that he had done.*

> (Genesis 24:67) ***And Isaac brought her into his mother Sarah's tent, and took Rebekah, and she became his wife; and he loved her:*** *and Isaac was comforted after his mother's death.*

Notice how in verse 67 Isaac brought Rebekah into his mother's tent. In like manner, Jesus will take us into the place that He has prepared for us in His Father's house (i.e. Heaven). It seems almost superfluous to say that Isaac did not take Rebekah back to her native Haran. We mention this because those who teach a post-Tribulation Rapture suggest that the Church will be caught up into the air to meet Jesus at His Second Coming and then be brought straight back down to Earth with Him. It is for this reason that some have, tongue in cheek, dubbed this the yo-yo Rapture. However, not only does this precious type not fit the post-Tribulation Rapture scenario, but the following words of Jesus also plainly contradict it.

> *(John 14:1) Let not your heart be troubled: ye believe in God, believe also in me.*
>
> *(John 14:2)* ***In my Father's house are many mansions****: if it were not so, I would have told you.* ***I go to prepare a place for you.***
>
> *(John 14:3) And if I go and prepare a place for you,* ***I will come again, and receive you unto myself; that where I am, there ye may be also.***

With these words, in the plainest manner possible, the Lord Jesus makes it very clear that when He comes for us at the Rapture it will be to take us back to Heaven as His Bride, where the consummation will take place. The Church will remain with Him in Heaven whilst the seven years of Tribulation are taking place on Earth.

Our third example is closely linked with the previous one. It concerns Rebekah herself.

REBEKAH A TYPE OF THE BRIDE OF CHRIST

1. *As Rebekah believed and yielded to the pleadings of* ***Eliezer****, so the Church believes and yields to the pleadings of the* ***HOLY SPIRIT****.*

2. *As Rebekah was willing to separate herself from her kinsfolk for* ***Isaac's sake, so*** *the Believer is willing to separate himself from his kinsfolk for* ***JESUS' SAKE.***

3. *As Eliezer on the way to Isaac told Rebekah all about his Master Isaac, and what was in store for her, so the Holy Spirit as we journey on our earthly pilgrimage tells us what is in store for us when we shall meet our Isaac -* ***JESUS.***

4. *As Rebekah was a* ***Gentile*** *bride, so the Church of Christ is a* ***GENTILE*** *Bride. While Rebekah was a kinswoman of Isaac, she was a Gentile, for while Abraham was the first Hebrew, his kinspeople were Gentiles, for the Jews are the descendants of Judah, the fourth son of Abraham's grandson Jacob.*

5. *As Rebekah did not have to pass through any tribulation before she left her home to go to Isaac, so the Church will not have to pass through* ***THE TRIBULATION*** *before meeting Jesus.*

6. *As Isaac left his home and went* ***out into the field*** *to meet Rebekah, so Jesus will* ***DESCEND FROM HEAVEN TO MEET HIS BRIDE, THE CHURCH, IN THE AIR.***

7. *As it was* ***"eventide"*** *when Isaac met Rebekah, so it will be the* ***EVENTIDE OF THIS DISPENSATION WHEN JESUS MEETS HIS CHURCH.***

Again, these beautiful parallels between Rebekah and the Church have much to say to us. However, it is number 5 that we are most concerned with.

The similarities in these types are clearly far too numerous to be coincidental. Bearing that in mind, if it was really the End Time Church's appalling destiny to go through the horrors of the seven year Tribulation period, could we not reasonably expect something analogous to this to feature within this type? Needless to say, it does not. There is not a word about some especially terrible period of upheaval in her homeland, which Rebekah would need to endure before departing with Eliezer.

Let us also consider Rebekah's journey with Eliezer, from her native Haran to the land of Canaan. In reality it was doubtless long, tiring and involving hardships and discomforts. It is not difficult to imagine Eliezer, along the way, encouraging and comforting Rebekah by unfolding to her the godliness, attractiveness and wealth of Isaac, her husband to be. Whilst all of these thoughts are very reasonable assumptions, the fact remains that we are not told anything at all about the journey in the Genesis chapter 24 narrative. However, could the journey be seen as a fitting analogy of both the whole of Church history as well as an individual believer's walk with the Lord up until the Rapture?

In summary, we have looked at three types that wonderfully foreshadow some aspect or other of the pre-Tribulation Rapture pattern. The reader is lovingly encouraged to search the Hebrew Scriptures for other examples, which will prove to be a great blessing. However, we cannot leave this precious subject without remarking how it tends to be either ignored or glossed over by those denying a pre-Tribulation Rapture. Further to this, we have yet to be shown a single type from the Hebrew Scriptures that foreshadows anything other than a pre-Tribulation Rapture format.

CHAPTER 6

EXPLAINING AWAY THE RAPTURE TO A DECEIVED WORLD

BEFORE WE BEGIN

If you are either newly saved or perhaps have not yet ventured beyond the 'milk' of God's Word, this chapter might seem like 'strong meat'. But may I encourage you to read Hebrews 5:12-14, praying that the Holy Spirit will open your eyes to the spiritual reality in these closing days of the present Age. If we are to become mature and effective disciples of the Lord Jesus Christ, we must take seriously the *whole* of God's Word and not just concentrate on the topics with which we are familiar. It is alarming how many Christians seem to be completely oblivious of Bible prophecy, either through wrong or even no teaching on the subject in their churches or, sadly, through lukewarm indifference. There is a ferocious battle being fought for the souls of men and women. An army that has little or no idea of what the enemy is up to is at best ineffective and at worst already defeated. How many in the modern Church have any true and experiential understanding of the following passage?

(Ephesians 6:10) Finally, my brethren, be strong in the Lord, and in the power of his might.

(Ephesians 6:11) ***Put on the whole armour of God****, that ye may be able to* ***stand against the wiles of the devil.***

(Ephesians 6:12) For ***we wrestle*** *not against flesh and blood, but* ***against principalities, against powers, against the rulers of the darkness of this world, against spiritual wickedness in high*** **[heavenly]** ***places.***

(Ephesians 6:13) Wherefore take unto you the ***whole armour of God,*** *that ye may* ***be able to withstand in the evil day****, and having done all, to stand.*

(Ephesians 6:14) Stand therefore, having your loins girt about with truth, and having on the breastplate of righteousness;

(Ephesians 6:15) And your feet shod with the preparation of the gospel of peace;

(Ephesians 6:16) Above all, taking the shield of faith, wherewith ye shall be able to quench all the fiery darts of the wicked [one].

(Ephesians 6:17) And take the helmet of salvation, and the sword of the Spirit, which is the word of God:

(Ephesians 6:18) Praying always with all prayer and supplication in the Spirit, and watching thereunto with all perseverance and supplication for all saints;

Whilst a large part of our spiritual warfare must be waged against our own sin, corruptions and temptations, we must also gain an intelligent understanding of what the Devil is using to deceive the multitudes, otherwise we will not be able to counter and expose it. The notion that *all* we need to understand is the Gospel itself is very naive. Of course the Gospel is absolutely central, but if we have little or no understanding of so much else that the Word of God gives light on (especially prophecy), we will be severely hampered in answering questions about what is going on in the world. This author is a street preacher and can testify to having had many conversations in which an accurate knowledge of Bible prophecy was crucial.

Nevertheless, a word of caution might be appropriate here. We are not suggesting for a minute that Christians should occupy themselves with delving into the deep and dark things of Satan's activities. An awareness of them is necessary, but a preoccupation with them is dangerous and to be avoided. Paul gets the balance right in the following words:

> *Lest Satan should get an advantage of us: for* ***we are not ignorant of his devices.*** *(2 Corinthians 2:11)*

Surely, one of the major problems in today's Church is that so many of us *are* ignorant of his devices.

SETTING THE SCENE

The likely world scenario in the aftermath of the Rapture has been the subject of much discussion and conjecture amongst prophetically aware Christians, not to mention certain movies that have been made on the subject. Whilst some aspects of the circumstances must remain speculative, we believe it is possible to make a reasonably accurate forecast based on the following considerations:

Biblical principles reveal the truth that God always rescues His redeemed people before He pours His righteous judgement upon the ungodly. In His grace and long-suffering, God gives plenty of warning of His intention to judge all those who have rejected Christ. The heart of man is unchanging in his sin, rebellion and wilful rejection of God's Word. If he rejects God's Word about his need of salvation then he will most certainly pay no heed to what God says about future events. Left to himself after a major event such as the Rapture has happened, he will also reject the truth about the precise nature and identity of the large body of missing people, as well as the real reason for the occurrence. It is extremely sobering to read 2 Thessalonians 2:8-12, concerning the revealing of *"that Wicked"* (or *"the lawless one"*), namely the Antichrist, after the Rapture. God Himself sends a *"strong delusion, that they should believe a lie"* upon an ungodly world population who *"believed not the truth, but had pleasure in unrighteousness"*.

The truth in the first point is all too easily observed in 21st-century Britain and the rest of the world. The majority of people have believed the lie of evolution and rejected God's Word, which reveals the truth about an originally perfect creation. This perfect creation was soon ruined by man's sin, resulting in God's curse upon the creation, but also the first gracious promise of the coming Redeemer. Nevertheless, only a few generations later *"...GOD saw that the wickedness of man was great in the earth, and that every imagination of the thoughts of his heart was only evil continually."* *(Genesis 6:5)*. No doubt this appalling situation had been drastically accelerated by the widespread genetic contamination of mankind, brought about by fallen angels *("the sons of God")*, as recorded in Genesis 6:1-4. Some have tried to find a more palatable interpretation of these verses by insisting that the *"sons of God"* were simply godly men who had married ungodly women. However, there are two major problems with that notion. Firstly, the phrase *"sons of God"* always refers to angelic beings in other parts of the Hebrew Scriptures (Old Testament). Secondly, the union of godly men with ungodly women does not produce abnormal offspring (giants). Therefore, the plain, grotesque meaning of Genesis 6:1-4 is clear. This then, was the extreme situation for which there was no solution but Noah's flood. At this point we should take serious note that the Lord Jesus spoke of the conditions in Noah's day, which led to the judgement of the Flood, being repeated just before He comes in judgement. *"And as it was in the days of Noe* [Noah], *so shall it be also in the days of the Son of man." (Luke 17:26).* Rejection of the truth concerning man's origins leads inevitably to rejection of the truth concerning his future. Many today scoff at the notion that God is about to arise in judgement upon this world and some of these claim to be Christians. To many, nothing could be more ridiculous than the teaching of the Rapture and subsequent Tribulation upon the Earth. Little do they realise that they are actually fulfilling these prophetic words:

> *(2 Peter 3:3) Knowing this first, that* ***there shall come in the last days scoffers****, walking after their own lusts,*
>
> *(2 Peter 3:4) And* ***saying, Where is the promise of his coming?*** *for since the fathers fell asleep, all things continue as they were from the beginning of the creation.*
>
> *(2 Peter 3:5) For this* ***they willingly are ignorant of****, that by* ***the word of God*** *the heavens were of old, and the earth standing out of the water and in the water:*
>
> *(2 Peter 3:6)* ***Whereby the world that then was, being overflowed with water, perished:***
>
> *(2 Peter 3:7) But the heavens and the earth, which are now,* ***by the same word*** *are kept in store,* ***reserved unto fire against the day of judgment and perdition of ungodly men.***

In a nutshell, modern man, having rejected the truth, has been set up to be taken completely by surprise and deceived by the sudden onset of soon-coming, awesome events. One trembles at the thought of being in their shoes.

Looking at trends in society over the last few decades and more recent developments, a very interesting picture emerges. When one's 'spiritual blinkers' are removed by the grace and mercy of God, it becomes obvious that all of these developments have been orchestrated. The 20th century witnessed an increasing appetite for science-fiction novels and movies, as well as those based on the occult and supernatural. The widespread modern deception that life on Earth has evolved has provided the ideal foundation for an even greater delusion. Man reasons that, if life evolved on Earth, then surely it must also have evolved in some form or other elsewhere in this vast universe. This is the basis for many science-fiction movies, such as HG Wells' "The War of the Worlds", "Close Encounters of the Third Kind", "Alien", "E.T. The Extra-Terrestrial" and "Independence Day" to name but a few. Whilst some readers might be sceptical about the modern UFO phenomenon, the detailed accounts from highly credible eye witnesses, such as military and commercial pilots and law enforcement officers, not usually given to hysteria or flights of fantasy, leaves little doubt that *something* is going on. There is a real expectation amongst many of making contact with extra-terrestrial life before very much longer. Huge sums of money and a lot of time are spent on things such as The Search for Extraterrestrial Intelligence (SETI) Institute. Even the Vatican has an observatory and is apparently searching for and expecting to make contact with alien life. Closely paralleling an appetite for all things extra-terrestrial has been a hunger for entertainment based on the occult and supernatural. This has spawned many very unpleasant movies over the years including some with the capacity to cause serious disturbance of mind in people. In more recent years we have witnessed an explosion in the popularity of the "Harry Potter" books and movies, which have served to glamorise and normalise witchcraft and the occult in the minds of the up-and-coming generation.

SEEING THE BIG PICTURE

Keeping in mind all of these observations, let us now seek to draw all the strands together in order to answer the question of how the Rapture is likely to be explained away by secular and religious authorities to a deceived world.

An important aspect of the likely scenario after the Rapture is often overlooked. We have already touched upon this matter in answering objection number 6 in chapter 3. From the world's perspective, it will not be obvious that the Church has gone. Why is this? It needs to be remembered that the world does not really comprehend the difference between true and merely nominal Christians. Indeed, most do not even *want* to know. In the world's estimation, all who 'go to church' or are, in their vague apprehension, 'religious', must be 'Christians'. Such willing ignorance will prove very costly indeed, resulting in the great majority being easily deceived.

We need to remember that the Lord Jesus Christ is coming for His Bride, the true Church, which is composed entirely and exclusively of all truly born-again believers. There will be none included in the Rapture who are Christian in name only. With huge numbers of professed 'Christians' left on Earth, including the papacy, much of the leadership and membership in the various Orthodox churches, Anglican and liberal Protestant denominations as well as many 'evangelical' and 'charismatic' churches, it will surely be very easy to claim that the 'church' is still on Earth.

Added to this is the apathy and increasingly hard-hearted hostility of the general populace towards the Gospel. This author, as a street preacher, can readily testify to this. We are often verbally abused and insulted by those who despise the Lord Jesus Christ and, by extension, His people. But perhaps most shocking of all is that some of the opposition to the open-air proclamation of the Gospel comes from religious people who claim to be Christians. Sadly, the reality is that many folk, both secular and religious, would be glad to see the back of us. Soberingly, their desire is likely to be realised in the near future, but their celebrations are going to be very short-lived.

A PRE-PLANNED DECEPTION

As the *"father of lies"*, Satan has duped mankind in every age with a variety of deceptions tailored to the desires of man's fallen nature, his worldview and expectations at any particular point in history. Whilst the Babylonian, Greek and Roman 'gods', elves, hobgoblins, leprechauns or other manifestations might have suited the Devil's purposes long ago, they certainly will not do for a space-age, sophisticated and scientifically aware generation. No, what is needed is a high-tech and clever stratagem, custom-made for a generation who are *"professing themselves to be wise"*. Enter the modern UFO phenomenon and the resultant belief of many that extra-terrestrial life probably exists, having evolved elsewhere. The way that the Devil is described in the following verse is very interesting:

> *Wherein in time past ye walked according to the course of this world, according to* ***the prince of the power of the air****, the spirit that now worketh in the children of disobedience:* (Ephesians 2:2)

Recently, some very illuminating documentaries have been produced, examining the whole UFO phenomenon in the light of God's Word. Eyewitness accounts of sightings as well as closer contacts or even alleged abductions by beings from UFOs are scrutinised. Many of the witnesses are highly credible and clearly have nothing to gain but, potentially, much to lose by sharing their stories. Some have evidently been highly traumatised by their experiences.

So are there any clues to the real identity of these supposed extra-terrestrials? Thankfully there are. It would appear that in many instances these 'extra-terrestrials' bring messages to humanity. Apparently these messages all bear a striking similarity to each other and follow a similar theme. They are supportive of New Age beliefs that mankind is being prepared for an evolutionary leap into a 'higher level of consciousness' in preparation for a 'wonderful new era'. They also denigrate the correct, Biblical understanding of who Jesus Christ is, claiming that He was no different to any of us but had simply learned the secret of tapping into the 'higher powers'. The messages are more or less the same as those obtained by mediums who, by channelling, have made contact with so-called Ascended Masters or similar.

In the documentary "The UFO Conspiracy" (New Liberty Videos, 2004), the late Dr John Weldon, one of many contributors, asked the following simple but penetrating questions:

"How credible is it to think that literally thousands of genuine extra-terrestrials would fly millions of light years simply to teach New Age philosophy, deny Christianity and support the occult? And why would the entities actually possess and inhabit people just like demons do if they were really advanced extra-terrestrials?"

To the discerning reader, there is really only one convincing answer to these questions. The so-called extra-terrestrials are in fact visible manifestations of demonic entities, controlled by Satan. Their purpose is to deceive mankind and prepare him for an even greater deception to come.

We need to remember that the Rapture will occur suddenly and without any prior warning signs. Much of the world population will be terrified, bewildered and in many cases grief stricken at the loss of loved ones. Ordinary people will demand and expect an answer from the authorities, both secular and religious. At the time of writing this book (prior to the Rapture) the stage is being set for the grand finale. At the moment, the 'Restrainer' (the Holy Spirit through the true Church) is preventing the total unleashing of the spirit of lawlessness, which is being kept within certain bounds. However, when the Rapture occurs *all* restraint upon evil will be removed.

> *(2 Thessalonians 2:6-7 RV) And now ye know that which* ***restraineth,*** *to the end that he may be revealed in his own season. For the mystery of lawlessness doth already work: only* ***there is one that restraineth now, until he be taken out of the way.***

In the verses that follow, we are given a sobering insight into what will start to take place on the Earth after the Rapture:

> *(2 Thessalonians 2:8) And then shall* ***that Wicked*** [i.e. the Antichrist] ***be revealed,*** *whom the Lord shall consume with the spirit of his mouth, and shall destroy with the brightness of his coming:*

> *(2 Thessalonians 2:9)* ***Even him, whose coming is after the***

working of Satan with all power and signs and lying wonders,

(2 Thessalonians 2:10) And with ***all deceivableness of unrighteousness in them that perish; because they received not the love of the truth, that they might be saved.***

(2 Thessalonians 2:11) And for this cause ***God shall send them strong delusion, that they should believe a lie:***

(2 Thessalonians 2:12) ***That they all might be damned*** [i.e. condemned] ***who believed not the truth, but had pleasure in unrighteousness.***

In these fearsomely sobering words, God is telling us what will befall the majority of those who, in the days before the Rapture, persistently rejected Jesus Christ and their need of salvation. Notice that, because all divine restraint will now have been removed, the Antichrist will be revealed and later accompanied by powerful, satanic displays of lying, supernatural signs and wonders. The most solemn aspect of this fearful scene is that it is God's righteous purpose in judgement to send this *"strong delusion"* upon a Christ-rejecting world. It is important to understand that this state of affairs has been a long time in the making. Over the last few decades the world has been becoming more and more godless, with militant atheism commonplace in modern Britain and the Western world. As people, including many who claim to be Christians, have rejected the truth about God, creation, mankind in sin and redemption in Jesus Christ, they have replaced it with the foundational lie of evolution. This has led to an increasing spirit of lawlessness and susceptibility to further intellectual and spiritual delusions such as belief in extra-terrestrials and other occult-based deceptions. All of this has made those who have scorned the truth absolutely ripe for Satan's counterfeit saviour, the Antichrist. At a time of world crisis and upheaval in the aftermath of the Rapture, people will be looking for a powerful leader to allay their fears, give them answers and provide world 'peace and security'. He is possibly alive somewhere in the world today, but will not be revealed until after the Rapture. Let us not underestimate the effect of the satanic power, signs and lying wonders, that will soon follow his revelation, upon so many who have for decades been feeding upon a diet of such things for their entertainment. One of his first remarkable acts will be to confirm or enforce a peace treaty between Israel and her surrounding enemies for a period of seven years. This will signal the beginning of the seven year Tribulation.

> *And* ***he*** [the Antichrist] ***shall confirm the covenant with many for one week*** [of years]*: and in the midst of the week he shall cause the sacrifice and the oblation to cease, and for the overspreading of abominations he shall make it desolate, even until the consummation, and that determined shall be poured upon the desolate.* *(Daniel 9:27)*

JOINING THE DOTS...

Many New Age and UFO cults expect and teach that, at some point in the near future, millions of people from around the world will be evacuated from the Earth. The details of how and why this will happen vary slightly between the different groups. However, the common thread is that millions of people will disappear from the face of the Earth without a trace. This information is not difficult to find on their various websites. Most make no attempt to hide the fact that their teaching has been channelled from so-called Ascended Masters or similar. Books on the same theme, such as "Project World Evacuation", have also been published. Whilst some readers might be tempted to brush these things off as being the fanciful notions of fringe groups, there is the very strong likelihood that they will become 'mainstream' almost overnight. How is this likely to happen?

We mentioned near the beginning of this chapter that the Vatican has a very keen interest in the whole matter of extra-terrestrial life and has an observatory engaged in searching for it. The current Pope has declared his belief in the 'Big Bang' and evolution, which he believes to be compatible with the Christian faith, which it most certainly is not. As we also mentioned earlier, evolution is the ideal foundation upon which to build the delusion that life has probably evolved elsewhere. As well as religious figures, there are also a considerable number of famous politicians, military commanders, scientists and astronauts who are thoroughly convinced that UFOs exist and some have seen them for themselves. Here are some examples to ponder:

From the Daily Telegraph online 22nd April 2009:

Are UFOs real? Famous people who believed.

The former NASA astronaut ***Edgar Mitchell*** *has claimed that aliens exist and their visits are being covered up by the United States government. Mitchell is in good company in his beliefs. Here we highlight 12* [we will not quote all 12] *other public figures who believe that extraterrestrials may have been visiting our planet over the last 100 years.*

Jimmy Carter*, US President from 1976 to 1980, promised while on the campaign trail that he would make public all documents on UFOs if elected. He said: "I don't laugh at people any more when they say they've seen UFOs. I've seen one myself."*

***General Douglas MacArthur**, the Korean and Second World War soldier, said in 1955 that "the next war will be an interplanetary war. The nations of the earth must someday make a common front against attack by people from other planets. The politics of the future will be cosmic, or interplanetary".*

***Monsignor Corrado Balducci**, a Vatican* **[note Vatican connection again]** *theologian, said: "Extraterrestrial contact is a real phenomenon. The Vatican is receiving much information about extraterrestrials and their contacts with humans from its embassies in various countries, such as Mexico, Chile and Venezuela."*

***Professor Stephen Hawking**: "Of course it is possible that UFOs really do contain aliens as many people believe, and the Government is hushing it up."*

***Air Chief Marshal Lord Dowding**, commander of RAF Fighter Command during the Battle of Britain: "I am convinced that these objects do exist and that they are not manufactured by any nations on earth."*

***Ronald Reagan**, US President from 1980 to 1988, "I looked out the window and saw this white light. It was zigzagging around. I went up to the pilot and said, 'Have you ever seen anything like that?' He was shocked and he said, 'nope.' And I said to him: 'Let's follow it!' We followed it for several minutes. It was a bright white light. We followed it to Bakersfield, and all of a sudden to our utter amazement it went straight up into the heavens. When I got off the plane I told Nancy all about it."*

***Mikhail Gorbachev**, the USSR's last head of state: "The phenomenon of UFOs does exist, and it must be treated seriously."*

***Richard Nixon**, US President from 1969 to 1974: "I'm*

not at liberty to discuss the government's knowledge of extraterrestrial UFOs at this time. I am still personally being briefed on the subject."

From the Daily Mail online 22 April 2015:

Governments are HIDING aliens, claims former defence minister: ***Paul Hellyer*** *urges world leaders to reveal 'secret files'.*

A former defence minister has accused world leaders of concealing the presence of aliens. Paul Hellyer, who was a Canadian [Defence] *Minister from 1963 to 1967, is now urging world powers to release what he believes to be hidden data on UFOs. 'Much of the media won't touch [the documents]', he said during a keynote speech at the Disclosure Canada Tour at the University of Calgary. 'You just have to keep working away and hope that someday you get a critical mass,' he said, according to a report by CTV. '[The public] will say, in one way or another, "Mr President or Mr Prime Minister we want the truth and we want it now because it affects our lives." Hellyer, 91, first went public with his belief in aliens on Earth in 2005, becoming the first high ranking politician to do so.*

BBC News website 15 February 2017:

"Winston Churchill's views on aliens revealed in lost essay.

A newly unearthed essay by Winston Churchill reveals he was open to the possibility of life on other planets.

In 1939, the year World War Two broke out, Churchill penned a popular science article in which he mused about the likelihood of extra-terrestrial life.

The 11-page typed draft, probably intended for a newspaper, was updated in the 1950s but never published.

In the 1980s, the essay was passed to a US museum, where it sat until its rediscovery last year.

The document was uncovered in the National Churchill Museum in Fulton, Missouri, by the institution's new director Timothy Riley. Mr Riley then passed it to the Israeli astrophysicist and author Mario Livio who describes the contents in the latest issue of Nature journal.

Churchill's interest in science is well-known: he was the first British prime minister to employ a science adviser, Frederick Lindemann, and met regularly with scientists such as Sir Bernard Lovell, a pioneer of radio astronomy."

All of the foregoing examples make compelling reading in our quest to 'join the dots'.

The timing of the unearthing of Winston Churchill's essay is interesting. When it is desired to influence the thinking of a population, it can be very effective to call forth the words of a great and highly respected figure from the past that appear to lend their support to a desired narrative.

However, the irony of Churchill's thinking about extra-terrestrial life is brought out by the following quote that reveals the depth of his respect for the Scriptures:

"We reject, however, with scorn all those learned and laboured myths that Moses was but a legendary figure upon whom the priesthood and the people hung their essential social, moral, and religious ordinances.

We believe that the most scientific view, the most up-to-date and rationalistic conception, will find its fullest satisfaction in

***taking the Bible story literally**, and in identifying one of the greatest of human beings with the most decisive leap forward ever discernible in the human story.*

We remain unmoved by the tomes of Professor Gradgrind and Dr. Dryasdust. We may be sure that all these things happened just as they are set out according to Holy Writ. We may believe that they happened to people not so very different from ourselves, and that the impressions those people received were faithfully recorded and have been transmitted across the centuries with far more accuracy than many of the telegraphed accounts we read of the goings-on of today.

In the words of a forgotten work of Mr. Gladstone, we rest with assurance upon 'The impregnable rock of Holy Scripture." (W.S. Churchill, "Moses: The Leader of a People" in Thoughts and Adventures (London 1932)

How do we account for Churchill's belief in the likelihood of extra-terrestrial life existing whilst also insisting that the Scriptures should be taken literally? The following extract from Mario Livio's article in the Nature journal of 15 February 2017 (referred to in the BBC News website article) provides a strong clue:

"Aged 22, while stationed with the British Army in India in 1896, he [Churchill] *read* **Darwin's "On the Origin of Species"** *and a primer on physics. In the 1920s and 1930s,* ***he wrote popular-science essays on topics such as evolution*** *and cells in newspapers and magazines."*

Let us again note the relevance and importance of the evolution connection. If one believes that life on Earth came about through chance, random processes and somehow evolved into human beings, then it is perfectly logical and consistent, on the basis of sheer probability, to believe that life is highly likely to have evolved elsewhere in this vast universe.

It has to be admitted that the Church of yesteryear was intimidated and 'wobbled' in the face of an apparently unassailable challenge to the authority of Scripture from the new 'science' of evolution. Many well-meaning Christians tried to accommodate the supposedly proven long ages into the Genesis account, which gave rise to things like the 'Gap Theory'. In this, the vast aeons of time required by evolution were inserted between the first two verses of Genesis chapter 1. However, without realising it, they had fatally undermined the truth that there was no death or bloodshed before Adam sinned. This in turn cast doubt upon the whole need of a coming Saviour who would deal with the awful consequences for mankind of Adam's sin. The Lord Jesus treated Genesis as literal history and so did all the apostles, so we would do well to do the same.

We are very blessed at the present time to benefit from the work of various creation ministries who have demonstrated the logical fallacy of the notion of evolution from the standpoints of many different scientific disciplines. They have shown that the evidence all around us is perfectly consistent with a literal interpretation of the book of Genesis. It is therefore sad to see that, despite the wealth of excellent material available, there are still professing Christians who compromise with evolution, thus doing enormous damage to the Gospel and their own understanding of the Word of God.

Therefore, coming back to the question of Winston Churchill's belief in the possibility of extra-terrestrial life, we can conclude that his thinking was strongly influenced by embracing the idea of evolution, apparently not having appreciated its incompatibility with God's revelation of man's true history.

Today, evolution is presented in the media and the education system as if it were a proven fact and dissenters are routinely ridiculed. Despite its inability to stand up under close scientific scrutiny, evolution is the belief system of choice for so many, particularly as man's rebellion against God crescendos in the closing days of this Age. As we said earlier, it is virtually a prerequisite, foundational deception upon which the powerful, post-Rapture delusion will be built. This brings us to our conclusion as to how the Rapture, which will involve the bodily removal of every true Christian from the Earth, is likely to be explained away by secular and religious authorities.

DISCLOSURE

Claims have long been made that, concerning the UFO phenomenon and contact with so-called extra-terrestrials, governments know far more than they are currently willing to disclose. Certainly, the candid assertion of former Canadian defence Minister, Paul Hellyer (quoted earlier) lends much credence to these claims. Further to this, the words we quoted earlier of so many very high-profile people are highly significant. Another interesting factor is that, at the time of writing (early 2018), there is considerably increased coverage in the media on the subject of extra-terrestrial life. No doubt this has been partly stimulated by the recent discovery of planets orbiting nearby stars, with speculation that some of these could be Earth-like. Could this be the final stage of a softening-up process (albeit unwittingly by most of those involved), designed to precondition the population in readiness for disclosure? Let us remember that within God's sovereign purpose, in this current dispensation, the whole unbelieving world is under the deceptive grip of Satan.

> *In whom* ***the god of this world*** [i.e. Satan] ***hath blinded the minds of them which believe not,*** *lest the light of the glorious gospel of Christ, who is the image of God, should shine unto them.* *(2 Corinthians 4:4)*

> *We know that we are of God, and* ***the whole world lieth in the evil one*** [i.e. Satan]. *(1 John 5:19 RV)*

This author believes that it is highly likely that a worldwide disclosure will be made by governments or perhaps the United Nations that UFOs are real, extra-terrestrials exist and that contact with them has been going on for some time. Such a disclosure could take place in the fairly near future and will no doubt be accompanied by some very convincing proof. Perhaps it will be explained that the time was not right to release such information in the past, but that the time has now come. We also believe that it will almost certainly be substantiated by the Vatican, who will give the 'religious' assurance that they had been expecting this and that it is not something to be feared but rather embraced by people of all faiths and none. One speaker recently remarked that such a disclosure would constitute a 'game changer' in terms of mankind's collective view of what constitutes ultimate reality.

So, at what point is this disclosure likely to take place? That is a very difficult question to answer with any certainty, although the following thoughts might help us to make an educated guess.

One can envisage considerable problems for the authorities if disclosure was to take place before the Rapture. Why do we say this? Simply because, although many in the Church are fast asleep concerning these things, there are a considerable number of Christians who have a good understanding of what is going on. Some of these have ministries that reach many thousands through written articles, videos and social media on the Internet. Can we imagine these remaining silent whilst a satanic deception of such enormous magnitude was being foisted upon their fellow men? Of course not. Also, private Christians without far-reaching ministries would be 'working overtime' to warn unsaved family and friends of the lies being told. Even given the fact that the world is not noted for paying attention to what we say, such concerted warnings would surely cause grievous damage to the intention of such a deception. Add to this the fact that Satan is not omniscient. Whilst he obviously realises that the Rapture is close, he does not know exactly when it will occur. Therefore, if disclosure was made before the Rapture, it might be made too far in advance of our departure, leaving us plenty of time to be warning people of the deception.

Bearing in mind the foregoing reasoning, it seems more likely that disclosure would take place very soon after the Rapture. In this way, responsibility for the disappearance of millions of people could be attributed to the extra-terrestrials and their UFOs. This would provide Satan and his counterfeit messiah with a compelling explanation with which to deceive the world's Christ-rejecting population. Perhaps the Antichrist will appear to be in league with the extra-terrestrials. He may even claim to have arranged for the removal and re-education of all the 'negative' people who were intolerant of the 'new morality', who called it sin and thereby hindered mankind's evolution into the 'new consciousness'. This is the sort of scenario that some of the New Age teaching envisages. Another possibility is that a terrified and bewildered world population will be afraid that there might be another mass snatching-up of people to who knows where. Perhaps next time, it might be them. The Antichrist would then be able to assure them that whoever gives their allegiance to him would be perfectly safe, as he has been appointed by the extra-terrestrials to lead the world into a 'golden new age'. We need to remember that the unbelieving world will not realise that this pretender is the Antichrist. Let us also remember that the Scriptures reveal another important player, the False Prophet, who will powerfully direct people's allegiance towards the Antichrist.

> *(Revelation 13:11) And I beheld* ***another beast*** [i.e. the False Prophet, see also Revelation 16:13, 19:20 and 20:10] *Coming up out of the earth; and he had two horns like a lamb, and he spake as a dragon.*

> *(Revelation 13:12) And he exerciseth all the power of the first beast before him,* ***and causeth the earth and them which dwell therein to worship the first beast,*** *whose deadly wound was healed.*

Many believe that the Pope in office at the time would be a very likely candidate for the False Prophet. Nevertheless, however the finer details actually transpire, the Antichrist will be seen by the multitudes as the saviour of mankind.

THE OBVIOUS QUESTION

This book has sought to defend the scriptural truth that the Rapture *must* occur before the seven year Tribulation period begins.

In this chapter we have seen how a very powerful deception has been constructed in advance of the Rapture, in order to give a false explanation for the missing millions of people after it occurs. It is a deception that, by its nature, is ready to be rolled out at a moment's notice.

The obvious question is this: If the true Church is destined to go through the Tribulation, as many modern Bible teachers are now saying, why would such a deception be necessary? After the seven year Tribulation had begun, true Christians would still be on Earth and there would be no missing millions to account for. The obvious answer is that Satan knows that the true Church has to be removed along with the restraint exercised by the Holy Spirit, before he can bring forth his counterfeit messiah, the Antichrist.

So we can see that Satan, 'the father of lies', has one lie with which to try and deceive the present generation of true Christians (i.e. that they will go through the Tribulation period) and another lie with which to deceive an unbelieving world after those same true Christians have departed! One Devil, with different lies for different people for different purposes. Let us not be among those who are deceived.

CHAPTER 7

TO GOD BE THE GLORY

***To God be the glory,** great things He hath done,*
So loved He the world that He gave us His Son,
Who yielded His life an atonement for sin,
And opened the life gate that all may go in.

Fanny J Crosby

THE GLORY OF GOD AND THE BRIDE OF CHRIST

Great things He has done truly and indeed, will yet do. If you are already a child of God, have you yet been enabled by the Holy Spirit, at least in some measure, to dive into that fathomless ocean of divine love that the Lord Jesus has for His Bride, the true Church, as well as for you individually?

'Tis mystery all! The Immortal dies!
Who can explore His strange design?
In vain the firstborn seraph tries
To sound the depths of love Divine!
'Tis mercy all! let earth adore,
Let angel minds inquire no more.

Charles Wesley

Have you contemplated the depth and purity of the love of our heavenly Bridegroom for His Bride as mirrored in the beautiful and tender language of the Song of Solomon?

(Song of Solomon 2:8) *The voice of my beloved! behold, he cometh leaping upon the mountains, skipping upon the hills.*

(Song of Solomon 2:9) *My beloved is like a roe or a young hart: behold, he standeth behind our wall, he looketh forth at the windows, shewing himself through the lattice.*

(Song of Solomon 2:10) ***My beloved spake, and said unto me, Rise up, my love, my fair one, and come away.***

(Song of Solomon 2:11) *For, lo, the winter is past, the rain is over and gone;*

(Song of Solomon 2:12) *The flowers appear on the earth; the time of the singing of birds is come, and the voice of the turtle is heard in our land;*

(Song of Solomon 2:13) *The fig tree putteth forth her green figs, and the vines with the tender grape give a good smell.* ***Arise, my love, my fair one, and come away.***

(Song of Solomon 2:14) ***O my dove, that art in the clefts of the rock,*** *in the secret places of the stairs,* ***let me see thy countenance, let me hear thy voice; for sweet is thy voice, and thy countenance is comely.***

Or how about Adam's words when he first saw Eve?

And Adam said, ***This is now bone of my bones, and flesh of my flesh****: she shall be called Woman, because she was taken out of Man.* (Genesis 2:23)

As an illustration of the mysterious and divine union between Christ and His Bride, the true Church, Adam's vital union with Eve is a wonderful figure. Have we sufficiently grasped the amazing union and oneness into which we, as members of His mystical body, have been brought with our Lord Jesus Christ and each other?

> ***Now ye are the body of Christ**, and members in particular.* (1 Corinthians 12:27)

Are we not very slow to comprehend and enter into the wonders of the love of Christ for us who believe on Him? Surely, it is our tendency to spiritual insensibility that prompted the apostle Paul to pray so earnestly for the Ephesian believers:

> (Ephesians 3:14) *For this cause I bow my knees unto the Father of our Lord Jesus Christ,*
>
> (Ephesians 3:15) *Of whom the whole family in heaven and earth is named,*
>
> (Ephesians 3:16) *That he would grant you, according to the riches of his glory, to be strengthened with might by his Spirit in the inner man;*
>
> (Ephesians 3:17) *That Christ may dwell in your hearts by faith; **that ye, being rooted and grounded in love,***
>
> (Ephesians 3:18) ***May be able to comprehend with all saints what is the breadth, and length, and depth, and height;***
>
> (Ephesians 3:19) ***And to know the love of Christ, which passeth knowledge,** that ye might be filled with all the fulness of God.*

Can any one of us, who have entered into a revelation of the love of Christ, entertain for a moment the senseless idea that the Lord Jesus intends to pour out His wrath upon that part of His own mystical body that is supposedly still on Earth as He opens the seal judgements of Revelation chapter 6? How can such a doctrine glorify God? In fact, the purpose of all false doctrine is ultimately to rob God of the glory due to His Name.

Let us leave aside for a moment the clear verdict of Scripture. Which seems more conducive to the glory of God? (1) That His people should be looking constantly and expectantly for His appearing or (2) that they should be preoccupied with this present, sin-sick world, looking for the appearance of the Antichrist? The answer is obvious.

THE GLORY OF GOD AND THE TRUTH

Truth, indeed the whole truth, is intimately and indivisibly connected with the glory of God, as we shall now seek to demonstrate.

> *Whether therefore ye eat, or drink, or* ***whatsoever ye do, do all to the glory of God.*** *(1 Corinthians 10:31)*

Clearly, if we are called to teach the Word of God, that would be included in the "*whatsoever ye do*" in the above verse, which must therefore be done to the glory of God. If we are teaching error in any particular area of doctrine, then God cannot be glorified by it. It might be objected that no man has a perfect grasp of the whole Word of God, so what is he to do? Surely the answer is that he should not teach on any point about which he is either uncertain or confused, until he has obtained the clear witness of the Holy Spirit as to the truth about that matter. The following verse illustrates how vitally important this is.

> ***If any man speak, let him speak as the oracles of God;*** *if any man minister, let him do it as of the ability which God giveth:* ***that God in all things may be glorified through Jesus Christ,*** *to whom be praise and dominion for ever and ever. Amen.* (1 Peter 4:11)

It has been rightly said that whatever God says or does glorifies His Name. If we belong to God, surely it should be *our* highest aim, in everything that we say and do, to glorify God and not ourselves, other men or systems of men. The above verse clearly exhorts us to walk in the light of that great principle. However, let us look more closely at the first part of the verse: *"If any man speak, let him speak as the oracles of God"*.

Here we have an exhortation to those men who believe that they are called to teach the Word of God to others. Notice how high the bar is set in terms of the doctrinal accuracy required of them: *"let him speak as the oracles of God"*. The *"oracles of God"* is a reference to the Hebrew Scriptures (Old Testament) but of course applies equally to the New Testament.

> *This is he, that was in the church in the wilderness with the angel which spake to him in the mount Sina, and with our fathers: who received* ***the lively oracles*** *to give unto us:* (Acts 7:38)

"... ***which is called "the oracles", because it came from God****, and contained his mind and will, and was* ***a sure and infallible declaration*** *of it; and "lively" ones, because delivered "viva voce", with an articulate voice, and in audible sounds, and because it is quick and powerful, sharper than a two-edged sword". (John Gill's commentary)*

So we see that God requires those who teach the Word of God, no matter the subject concerned, to *"speak as the oracles of God"*. For what purpose? *"that God... may be glorified through Jesus Christ"*. Clearly, God is glorified when the truth is taught about any particular aspect of His Word. Conversely, He is dishonoured and robbed of the glory due to His Name when error of any kind is taught and tolerated.

Perhaps it would help us to remember that the Lord Jesus Christ *is* the truth.

> *Jesus saith unto him,* ***I am*** *the way,* ***the truth****, and the life: no man cometh unto the Father, but by me.* *(John 14:6)*

How much of the truth is Jesus? Is He some of the truth, most of the truth or the truth in its entirety? No true Christian should have any difficulty in affirming that the Lord Jesus is the truth in its entirety. We know that God is glorified in the Lord Jesus Christ as verses such as the following clearly teach:

> *Therefore, when he was gone out, Jesus said, Now is the Son of man glorified,* ***and God is glorified in him.*** *(John 13:31)*

Since God is glorified in Jesus, it follows that He is glorified in the truth, because Jesus is the truth. Again we must emphasise that God requires *the whole truth* to be taught, not some of it or even most of it, but all of it. Surely that is why there are so many exhortations in the Scriptures to preach the *whole* counsel of God. Notice the prevalence of the word, *'all'*, in the following examples:

> *Thus saith the LORD; Stand in the court of the LORD'S house, and speak unto all the cities of Judah, which come to worship in the LORD'S house,* ***all the words that I command thee*** *to speak unto them;* ***diminish not a word:*** *(Jeremiah 26:2)*

Moreover he said unto me, Son of man, ***all my words that I shall speak unto thee*** *receive in thine heart, and hear with thine ears.* (Ezekiel 3:10)

Teaching them to observe ***all things whatsoever I have commanded you:*** *and, lo, I am with you alway, even unto the end of the world. Amen.* (Matthew 28:20)

Then he said unto them, O fools, and slow of heart to believe ***all that the prophets have spoken:*** (Luke 24:25)

And beginning at Moses and all the prophets, he expounded unto them in ***all the scriptures*** *the things concerning himself.* (Luke 24:27)

Go, stand and speak in the temple to the people ***all the words of this life.*** (Acts 5:20)

For I have not shunned to declare unto you ***all the counsel of God.*** (Acts 20:27)

Not only are we to teach the whole counsel of God, but we are to teach it correctly, rightly dividing it, not twisting and misusing it to support our own theories or preferences.

Study to shew thyself approved unto God, a workman that needeth not to be ashamed, ***rightly dividing the word of truth.*** (2 Timothy 2:15)

C H Spurgeon well understood these principles as evidenced by the following extract from his commentary on the first verse of Psalm 115.

Not unto us, O LORD, not unto us, but ***unto thy name give glory****, for thy mercy, and* ***for thy truth's sake.*** (Psalms 115:1)

We may not desire the triumph of our opinions, for our

own sakes, or for the honour of a sect, but we may confidently pray for ***the triumph of truth, that God Himself may be honoured*** [i.e. glorified].

(C H Spurgeon's "The Treasury of David")

In Paul's exhortation to the young Timothy *(2 Timothy 2:15)*, it is implicit that it *is* possible to be a workman who will be ashamed when, at the judgement seat of Christ, the Lord examines what he taught and why he taught it. If this is not the case, then Paul's appeal to Timothy to study the Word *and* rightly divide it would not be necessary. It must be emphasised that we are dealing here with the case of a true believer teaching error and not an unsaved apostate who denies the Lord and His Word. Is this not why we are given another warning in the following verse?

Be not many teachers, my brethren, knowing that we shall receive heavier judgment. (James 3:1 RV)

In commenting on this warning, the late Dr J Vernon McGee said the following:

"James is saying that a teacher has a greater responsibility, and the reason for that is ***the grave danger of teaching the wrong thing.*** *I am absolutely amazed and overwhelmed at the way* ***so many Christian folk fall for all kinds of teaching, particularly that which has to do with prophecy.*** *...They need to* ***know more of the Word of God than they do."***

"The ease with which ***people fall for their teachings*** *has ministered to* ***a great deal of conceit and pride on the part of many teachers."***

Before we move on to apply these vital principles of truth

to the whole matter of the Rapture, let us also examine what the Word teaches concerning the Holy Spirit and truth.

> *Even* ***the Spirit of truth;*** *whom the world cannot receive, because it seeth him not, neither knoweth him: but ye know him; for he dwelleth with you, and shall be in you.* (John 14:17)

> *But when the Comforter is come, whom I will send unto you from the Father, even* ***the Spirit of truth,*** *which proceedeth from the Father, he shall testify of me:* (John 15:26)

> *Howbeit when he,* ***the Spirit of truth,*** *is come, he will guide you into* ***all truth:*** *for he shall not speak of himself; but whatsoever he shall hear, that shall he speak: and he will shew you things to come.* (John 16:13)

> *This is he that came by water and blood, even Jesus Christ; not by water only, but by water and blood. And it is the Spirit that beareth witness, because* ***the Spirit is truth.*** (1 John 5:6)

In these passages we learn that the Holy Spirit is also truth. This should not surprise us because the Hebrew Scriptures also clearly teach that our God is the God of truth:

> *He is the Rock, his work is perfect: for all his ways are judgment:* ***a God of truth*** *and without iniquity, just and right is he.* (Deuteronomy 32:4)

> *Into thine hand I commit my spirit: thou hast redeemed me, O* ***LORD God of truth.*** (Psalms 31:5)

> *That he who blesseth himself in the earth shall bless himself in* ***the God of truth;*** *and he that sweareth in the earth shall swear by* ***the God of truth;*** *because the*

former troubles are forgotten, and because they are hid from mine eyes. (Isaiah 65:16)

Although a true Christian knows instinctively through the indwelling Holy Spirit that God is the God of truth, these passages of Scripture demonstrate beyond all doubt that God, in the tri-unity of His Persons, Father, Son and Holy Spirit, is truth.

THE GLORY OF GOD AND THE TRUTH ABOUT THE RAPTURE

Many believers seem unable to see straightforward logic when dealing with issues such as the timing of the Rapture. What do we mean by this? Ultimately, there are only two possibilities* for the true Church. Either she will be taken up to Heaven at the Rapture *before* the seven year Tribulation period begins or she will remain on Earth and go *into* the Tribulation. Clearly, the two possibilities *cannot both be true.* (*We are not concerned here with variations as to whether the Church supposedly goes through some or all of the Tribulation since, either way, the essential aspect of *imminence* is destroyed.)

Logically, one of these positions must be true and the other one must be false. However, at various prophecy teaching meetings around the country, one month an itinerant speaker will teach that the Rapture must occur before the Tribulation and the next month another will either teach or imply that the Church is destined to go into the Tribulation. In both cases, some in the audience will nod in approval and say 'amen', seemingly oblivious to the fact that the two teachings are totally contradictory and have enormously different implications! If it was not for one critical factor, it would be amazing that an issue of such simplicity should cause so much confusion for so many. What is that critical factor? Clearly, it is *spiritual opposition.* We know that *"God is not the author of confusion"* from 1 Corinthians 14:33. One does not have to have spent long teaching the pre-Tribulation Rapture before becoming aware of an intensity of opposition to it that is beyond the merely human.

We have already seen that God is glorified in the truth, which necessarily means that He cannot be glorified by false teaching of any kind. Surely, when it comes to things such as these, we should ask ourselves some searching questions. Are we *really* concerned for God's glory? If so, are we hungry for the *whole* truth that is revealed in His Word?

It is sometimes asked how we are to know which teaching on the Rapture is correct, since good men teach contradictory positions on the issue. The first thing to say is that we can be perfectly sure that the Holy Spirit (the Spirit of truth and Author of the Scriptures) has not led men into contradictory doctrinal positions over the Rapture or any other teaching for that matter. If men are in error, they have not been led there by the Holy Spirit. In spite of this, we are not to judge men's hearts as we are most certainly not competent to do so. However, we *are* to judge what they teach.

How can we judge teaching on the Rapture and avoid being *"...carried about with every wind of doctrine..." (Ephesians 4:14)*? Firstly, are we willing to ask God to examine our own hearts (Psalm 139:23-24) to determine whether we have any hidden motive, such as being too deeply rooted in this present world, which might tend to make us prefer a delay in the Lord's coming for us? Could it be that, even unconsciously, we have a deep seated 'salvation by works' leaven at work within ourselves? Perhaps we are afraid of the venomous attacks being made upon those who hold to the pre-Tribulation Rapture. Secondly, do we faithfully make our own diligent study of God's Word with a genuine hunger for the truth? If our hearts are in the right place and we are hungry for and seeking the truth, desiring to glorify God by believing and walking in the light of the truth, we meet the conditions for some precious promises.

> *(Luke 11:9) And I say unto you,* ***Ask, and it shall be given you; seek, and ye shall find; knock, and it shall be opened unto you.***

> *(Luke 11:10) For* ***every one that asketh receiveth;*** *and* ***he that seeketh findeth;*** *and* ***to him that knocketh it shall be opened.***

C H Spurgeon clearly understood this vital principle, as revealed by his illuminating commentary on John 16:13.

> *Howbeit when he, the* ***Spirit of truth,*** *is come,* ***he will guide you into all truth:*** *for he shall not speak of himself; but whatsoever he shall hear, that shall he speak: and he will shew you things to come. (John 16:13)*

Truth is like a vast cavern into which we desire to enter, but we are not able to traverse it alone. At the entrance it is clear and bright; but if we would go further and explore its innermost recesses, we must have a guide, or we shall lose ourselves. ***The Holy Spirit, who knows all truth perfectly, is the appointed guide of all true believers,*** *and* ***He conducts them as they are able to bear it,*** *from one inner chamber to another, so that they behold the deep things of God, and His secret is made plain to them. What a promise is this for the humbly inquiring mind! We desire to know the truth and to enter into it. We are conscious of our own aptness to err, and we feel the urgent need of a guide. We rejoice that the Holy Spirit is come and abides among us.*

He condescends to act as a guide to us, and we gladly accept His leadership. ***"All truth" we wish to learn, that we may not be one-sided and out of balance. We would not be willingly ignorant of any part of revelation lest thereby we should miss blessing or incur sin.*** *The Spirit of God has come that He may guide us into all truth:* ***let us with obedient hearts hearken to His words and follow His lead.***

(C H Spurgeon's "Cheque Book of the Bank of Faith" 6th October reading)

Could anybody disagree with Mr Spurgeon on this matter? Indeed, the Lord Jesus Himself gives it His stamp of approval in the very next verse:

> ***He shall glorify me:*** *for he shall receive of mine,* ***and shall shew it unto you.*** *(John 16:14)*

Here again, in the words of the Lord Jesus, we see God's glory vitally connected with the truth. But how much truth? Clearly, the only satisfactory answer is *the whole truth,* since Jesus *is* the Truth.

FINAL EXHORTATION

There is a special crown reserved for those believers who have looked for, longed for and loved the appearing of our Lord Jesus Christ.

> *Henceforth there is laid up for me a crown of righteousness, which the Lord, the righteous judge, shall give me at that day:* ***and not to me only, but unto all them also that love his appearing.*** *(2 Timothy 4:8)*

Dear reader, let us covet that crown and join our voices together with the Holy Spirit in the following words:

And the Spirit and the bride say, Come. And let him that heareth say, Come. And let him that is athirst come. And whosoever will, let him take the water of life freely. (*Revelation 22:17*)

Let us look for and long for our soon-coming departure to be with our Lord Jesus who will receive us joyfully unto Himself.

(*Jude 1:24*) *Now unto him that is able to keep you from falling, and to present you faultless before the presence of **his glory** with exceeding joy,*

(*Jude 1:25*) *To the only wise God our Saviour, **be glory** and majesty, dominion and power, both now and ever. Amen.*

GLORY TO GOD IN THE HIGHEST!

APPENDIX 1

WHAT IS THE GOSPEL AND SALVATION?

The Ultimate Question

There is no more urgent question to settle than this for every man, woman and child on the planet. Concerns about such things as money, housing, food, clothing, education and careers, although important, all pale into insignificance against the ultimate question of where we will spend eternity.

The tragedy is that, particularly in the West, so few people are even asking the question. Many today do not believe that they will have a conscious existence after death, whereas the Bible makes it abundantly clear that death is neither the cessation of existence nor consciousness. We have an eternal soul that will remain fully conscious after death and go to either Heaven or Hades (often translated, "*Hell*"). There it will await a glorious, literal and physical resurrection in the case of God's people or an inglorious, literal and physical resurrection to stand judgement before God's throne in the case of the lost. Not many generations ago, a much larger proportion of the population had at least *some* understanding of this sobering truth.

God as Creator Denied

What has happened to render our generation so extraordinarily insensible to eternal matters? The answer lies in a wholesale shift of worldview that has increased its grip over each succeeding generation. Prior to that, the majority of people realised that there must be a Creator God, even if they did not profess to be Christian. What could account for such a dramatic change in worldview?

Ever since the modern theory of evolution was introduced by Darwin in 1859 as an alternative explanation for the origin of living organisms, including ourselves, it has gained increasing acceptance in the minds of today's men and women. It is now presented as science, which is very appealing to the many who desire to give their unbelief in God an 'intellectual' legitimacy. In recent decades many scientists have exposed the fatal flaws and futility of evolutionary thinking and shown that it is not really science at all, but should more accurately be described as a philosophy or even a religion. Despite this, it is pushed relentlessly in our educational establishments and the media. Well-known names like Richard Dawkins and David Attenborough act as the 'high priests' of this anti-God religion. Dissenters are ridiculed mercilessly and enormous efforts are made to ensure that powerful evidence supporting the Biblical account of creation is suppressed in the public arena. It is a great mercy of God that various creation ministries have been set up to make widely available the scientific evidence for creation and to expose the illogical and even fraudulent pseudo-science of evolution. However, the Bible makes it quite clear that even without the detailed evidence available from such ministries, the existence of the visible creation around us is quite sufficient to prove the existence of God.

For the invisible things of him from the creation of the world are clearly seen, being understood by the things that are made, even his eternal power and Godhead; so that ***they are without excuse****:* *(Romans 1:20)*

Without excuse! That is precisely how God views the multitudes of men and women in this generation who either deny His existence or make only a nominal acknowledgement of Him. The Word of God does not soft-pedal in its description of such people:

The fool *hath said in his heart, There is no God. They are corrupt, they have done abominable works, there is none that doeth good.* *(Psalms 14:1)*

Professing themselves to be wise, ***they became fools****,* *(Romans 1:22)*

If ever there was a generation that professed to be wise, and yet in reality were fools, it is ours. The inevitable result of evolutionary brainwashing over the last one and a half centuries is a modern generation that has lost virtually all God-consciousness. A consequence of this is loss of any sense of accountability for our actions in this life. This inevitably leads to a climate of increasing lawlessness and moral decay from the lowest in society to those holding high office. Our nation has been plumbing the depths of sin for many years now. In 1967 the murder of unborn children was legalised with the Abortion Act. Since then the downhill slide has accelerated to the point where our Government now believes that it has the authority to redefine marriage in opposition to God's clear definition of that institution. There are even many claiming to be Christians who support such wilful rebellion against God, thus unwittingly fulfilling the very End Time Bible prophecies that they refuse to take seriously.

The Bible is the Word of God

The Bible declares itself to be the Word of God.

All scripture is given by inspiration of God, and is profitable for doctrine, for reproof, for correction, for instruction in righteousness: (2 Timothy 3:16)

For the prophecy came not in old time by the will of man: but holy men of God spake as they were moved by the Holy Ghost. (2 Peter 1:21)

There is overwhelming evidence to support that the Bible is exactly what it claims to be. Unbeknown to most people, there are many artefacts in the British Museum that confirm the historical accuracy of much of the Old Testament (Hebrew Scriptures). There is also very impressive manuscript evidence for the New Testament. In fact, from a variety of disciplines such as mathematics and science there is more than enough evidence to corroborate the veracity of the Bible for any *honest* enquirer. Perhaps the most impressive evidence, though, lies in the extraordinary accuracy with which many specific prophecies have been fulfilled. The first advent and subsequent ministry of the Lord Jesus Christ fulfilled with one hundred percent accuracy numerous Old Testament prophecies concerning Him. It has been demonstrated many times that the probability of one man fulfilling all of these prophecies by chance is effectively zero.

The unfulfilled prophecies of the Bible are mainly concerned with events that will bring this present Age to a close. This will culminate in the Second Coming of the Lord Jesus Christ to save Israel from destruction at the hands of the world's armies and to set up the kingdom of God on Earth. Again, these prophecies are very detailed. For the first time in mankind's history, *all* of the ingredients needed for the fulfilment of these prophecies are in place. Before 1948, there was no nation of Israel for the Lord Jesus Christ to return to. Today, 70 years later, the Jewish nation exists, amidst much clamour and opposition. 'Natural' disasters and earthquakes are increasing exponentially in frequency, sexual immorality is rife, homosexual and transgender ideology is forced upon society, nations are losing their sovereignty to a world government plan and much of the professing church is hopelessly compromised with regard to the truth of the Bible. All of these signs are very clear indicators that the end of this present Age is upon us. Sadly, many choose to remain ignorant of these things. However, burying our heads in the sand will not absolve us from our responsibility to respond to and obey the Gospel.

Why have we been so emphatic about the Bible being the Word of God? Simply because God's message of salvation (i.e. the Gospel) and true Christianity are defined solely by the Word of God and not by any church, tradition, theological college, clergyman or pastor. Much less is it defined by the Vatican, the Watchtower or any other cult headquarters. It is getting increasingly difficult in our day to find a church that faithfully preaches God's way of salvation. Even among those that do, many are blind to the obvious signs that the Second Coming of the Lord Jesus is drawing near because they fail to take Bible prophecy literally. Too many of today's churches should have a large spiritual health warning on their noticeboards. It is tragic to see multitudes deceived into thinking that they are in a right standing with God whilst they attend apostate churches or cults such as the Jehovah's Witnesses and willingly imbibe a message that cannot save anyone. In all likelihood, the majority will find out too late that they are still in their sins as God's judgement overtakes them. Many remain in such churches despite having been warned of the danger. The Bible gives the reason for this:

(2 Timothy 4:1) *I charge thee therefore before God, and the Lord Jesus Christ, who shall judge the quick and the dead at his appearing and his kingdom;*

(2 Timothy 4:2) ***Preach the word****; be instant in season, out of season; reprove, rebuke, exhort with all longsuffering and doctrine.*

(2 Timothy 4:3) ***For the time will come when they will not endure sound doctrine****; but after their own lusts shall they heap to themselves teachers, having itching ears;*

(2 Timothy 4:4) ***And they shall turn away their ears from the truth, and shall be turned unto fables.***

This prophecy from the Bible is being fulfilled with alarming rapidity in our day. Even within some of the so-called 'evangelical' church, false teachers tickle the ears of professing Christians with what they want to hear rather than what they need to hear. Far too few churches teach faithfully the truth about creation and refute evolution, declare unequivocally that Jesus Christ is the *only* way of salvation and warn people of the significance of the signs all around us that point to the nearness of His return. The Bible is the sole authority for true Christian faith and we follow the crowd in doubting it or departing from it at our peril.

The True History of Man

Man was created; he did not evolve. The widespread and aggressive denial of this truth is a foundational component of the wholesale departure from the Faith that is so clearly prophesied in the Bible for the closing days of this Age. If you want to be saved from the coming judgement of God, you will need to stop listening to the 'wisdom' of men, whether secular or 'religious', and start listening to what God has said in His Word.

The Genesis account of creation and the early history of mankind are to be taken literally, whatever today's scoffers may be saying. The Lord Jesus Christ Himself affirmed this:

> *And he answered and said unto them,* ***Have ye not read****, that* ***he which made them at the beginning*** *made them male and female,* (Matthew 19:4)

In these words to the unbelieving Pharisees, the Lord Jesus refers them to the book of Genesis, which He uses as being authoritative. In another exchange with the religious hierarchy, He said the following:

> (John 5:46) *For had ye believed Moses, ye would have believed me: for he wrote of me.*
>
> (John 5:47) *But* ***if ye believe not his writings, how shall ye believe my words?***

The potency of Jesus' words here should not be overlooked. Moses wrote the book of Genesis as he was led by the Holy Spirit. The Lord Jesus is effectively telling His hearers that if they do not believe Moses' writings, they will not be able to believe His words. This throws an interesting light on many a modern church which claims to be following the Lord Jesus Christ, whilst denying His Word about origins in Genesis. We need to be careful which 'Jesus' we are following: the true, Biblical Jesus or a 'Jesus' that suits our own preferences.

> (2 Corinthians 11:3) *But I fear, lest by any means,* ***as the serpent beguiled Eve through his subtilty****, so your minds should be corrupted from the simplicity that is in Christ.*

(2 Corinthians 11:4) For if he that cometh preacheth ***another Jesus****, whom we have not preached, or if ye receive* ***another spirit****, which ye have not received, or* ***another gospel****, which ye have not accepted, ye might well bear with him.*

Notice how the Apostle Paul treats Genesis as literal history in his reference to Eve being deceived by the serpent. He goes on to warn of the very real danger of following 'another Jesus' by sitting under the ministry of a false teacher. Is it really likely that those modern church leaders who deny the literal historicity of Genesis are wiser than the Lord Jesus Christ and the Apostle Paul?

Please read the early chapters of Genesis and receive them with strong faith. The good news of salvation through the Lord Jesus Christ makes no sense at all unless the early history of mankind as recorded in Genesis is literally true. Adam and Eve were created perfect and lived in a perfect environment where there was no suffering, death or bloodshed, but they soon failed the only moral test God put before them. Their fall into sin was our fall. The Bible is emphatic that death was not a part of the original creation; it came in solely as a consequence of sin. We are all born into this world as sinners because of the fact of 'original sin'. We are incapable of fully obeying God's perfect Law, even if we wanted to. The evidence of this is plain to see as we watch the news night after night or observe how children turn out who have not been trained and disciplined to restrain the natural tendency to selfishness and wrongdoing that is in them. We have all broken and continue to break God's Law for which there is a very real and terrifying penalty to pay. Many today are hardly affected when they are told this because they have become anaesthetized to the fear of God. Their minds have been darkened and blinded from years of accepting an entirely false worldview; a worldview that seeks to explain away the creation around us without a Creator. As we saw earlier in this appendix, the Bible teaches that the visible creation makes it obvious that there must be a Creator God, leaving men and women without excuse.

Spotlight on Man's Number One Problem

In our national life we expect our judges and magistrates to mete out appropriate punishments for lawbreakers. If they do not, there is a public outcry because justice has not been done. How strange it is then, that when it comes to breaking God's Law, we imagine that it should be entirely different. One popular notion is that as long as our 'good' deeds outweigh our bad deeds all will be well. By applying that thinking to the court room situation, someone guilty of armed robbery might escape jail by pointing to their many charitable works before and after the crime. We can all readily see the absurdity of that hypothetical scenario. There is a penalty for armed robbery and no amount of 'good' works prior to or following the offence makes any difference to the perpetrator's guilt.

The principle is the same, but to an infinitely higher degree, with God's laws that we have all broken. It is a solemn thing to break the law of the land, but who can begin to estimate the awful predicament of those who have broken the Law of the God who created the universe and everything in it? This God is holy, which means that He is set apart from and far above sinful mankind. He is perfect purity and righteousness; He is light and in Him is no darkness at all.

So just how many of us have broken God's Law? God gives us the answer in His Word:

> *For **all have sinned**, and come short of the glory of God;*
> *(Romans 3:23)*

Many of us today deceive ourselves as to our true nature, by comparing ourselves with others. We reason that because we may not have murdered, raped, robbed a bank or committed adultery, we are basically 'good' people. Our fatal mistake is our definition of the word 'good'. We give it a meaning that enables us to feel at ease with ourselves. God has a very different definition of the word 'good'.

(Matthew 19:16) And, behold, one came and said unto him, ***Good*** *Master* [teacher], ***what good thing shall I do****, that I may have eternal life?*

(Matthew 19:17) And he [Jesus] *said unto him, Why callest thou me* ***good? there is none good but one, that is, God****: but if thou wilt enter into life, keep the commandments.*

In this exchange between the Saviour and the 'Rich Young Ruler', Jesus corrects his understanding of the word 'good' and teaches that it can only be rightly applied to God. The following further quotes from the Scriptures clearly teach that true goodness is not to be found in anyone other than God.

(Romans 3:10) As it is written, ***There is none righteous, no, not one:***

(Romans 3:11) There is none that understandeth, there is none that seeketh after God.

(Romans 3:12) They are all gone out of the way, they are together become unprofitable; ***there is none that doeth good, no, not one.***

To be acceptable to God we need to be good, which, in its true definition, means total perfection. We have just read that there is not a single person on this planet that meets that standard. This is the bad news and it could hardly be worse. Until we are ready to admit that we are helpless sinners deserving of God's punishment, we will remain in our sins with the certain prospect of God's judgement ahead of us. If we refuse to believe the bad news about our sin, we will reject the good news of God's message of salvation.

God's Solution to our Problem

We have all sinned against an infinite and holy God by breaking His Law. The penalty for this is also infinite.

For the wages of sin is death (Romans 6:23a)

We have already seen that death is not the cessation of being. The penal death spoken of in this verse means a conscious existence banished from Heaven in a place of eternal torment and misery often translated in our Bible as Hell. Because God is a righteous Judge, He *must* judge sin in order to be consistent with His holy nature. Clearly, we are unable to pay the penalty for sin, so how can a righteous God save us from such an awful doom?

This is where the wonderful message of God's grace and mercy comes in. Before the foundation of the world, God had a plan to rescue men and women from their foreseen ruin in sin. As we have already seen, for a sinner to go free, the righteous penalty of the Law must be paid. If we cannot pay that price, where will the payment come from?

> *But* ***he was wounded for our transgressions, he was bruised for our iniquities:*** *the chastisement of our peace was upon him; and with his stripes we are healed.* (Isaiah 53:5)

This amazing prophecy is taken from the book of Isaiah in the Old Testament, which was all that existed of the Bible when Jesus was on Earth, because the New Testament had not yet been written. Isaiah chapter 53 contains a breathtakingly accurate prophecy of the death of the Lord Jesus Christ and the reason for it. It was written more than 700 years before He was born into this world as a man. When the New Testament verse below says, "*in accordance with the Scriptures*", it is referring to the above prophecy. Bible prophecy is one hundred percent accurate and has been described as "History written in advance". Clearly none but God alone can foretell the future in great detail and with total accuracy. The Bible clearly teaches that God is its author in such passages as 2 Timothy 3:16 and 2 Peter 1:20-21. Fulfilled prophecy is one of the most potent proofs that the Bible is indeed the Word of God.

> ***Christ died for our sins*** *in accordance with the Scriptures (1 Corinthians 15:3b)*

Here are some further verses dealing with this same, vital matter:

> *So* ***Christ was once offered to bear the sins of many;*** *and unto them that look for him shall he appear the second time without sin unto salvation. (Hebrews 9:28)*

> ***Who his own self bare our sins in his own body on the tree,*** *that we, being dead to sins, should live unto righteousness: by whose stripes ye were healed. (1 Peter 2:24)*

> ***For Christ also hath once suffered for sins, the just for the unjust, that he might bring us to God,*** *being put to death in the flesh, but quickened by the Spirit: (1 Peter 3:18)*

In these verses we are told the astonishing truth that Jesus Christ has died for *our* sins. Putting it another way, Jesus Christ became our substitute, dying the death that should rightfully be ours when he died on the cross nearly 2000 years ago. This has always been God's plan to save men and women from judgement. Perhaps the best known of all Bible verses puts it like this:

> *For God so loved the world, that he gave his only begotten Son, that whosoever believeth in him should not perish, but have everlasting life.* (John 3:16)

We should not just skim quickly through these words but read them *very carefully*, seeking to understand what God is saying to us through them. God's love for mankind is the reason that, in an act of pure grace, He sent His Son down to earth to lay down His life for the sins of the whole world. As a result, those who believe on Jesus Christ will not perish but have everlasting life. To perish is not merely a reference to physical death, but to eternal conscious punishment in Hell. Before moving on further we must understand what is meant by the grace of God. Grace in that sense can best be described as undeserved favour. When we are saved by trusting or believing on the Lord Jesus Christ, we are saved by grace.

> (Ephesians 2:8) *For* ***by grace*** *are ye saved* ***through faith****; and that not of yourselves: it is the gift of God:*

> (Ephesians 2:9) ***Not of works****, lest any man should boast.*

That we can be saved by the grace of God is the most wonderful news imaginable. Consider carefully for a few moments that Jesus Christ, the Son of the living God, has already paid the full penalty for your sin and mine when He died on the cross. There is nothing at all that can be added to the price He has paid, which is why the second verse above says *"Not of works"*. This means that it is absolutely impossible to earn your salvation with 'good' works. The very moment we simply turn in faith to Him for the forgiveness of our sins, we shall be saved.

> (Acts 16:30b) *Sirs, what must I do to be saved?*

> (Acts 16:31) *And they said,* ***Believe on the Lord Jesus Christ, and thou shalt be saved****, and thy house.*

So we see that salvation is a free gift from God that cannot be earned by working for it or obtained by trusting in church membership or religious rituals of any kind. God's wonderful way of salvation can seem too good to be true, yet it *is* true.

One would think that such an offer would be taken up immediately by people in their millions. Yet the reality is that, particularly in the West, very few people are being saved. Such is the darkness that has enveloped people's minds that they have become blind to the obvious. As we said at the beginning of this appendix, once people deny God as the Creator, further folly quickly ensues and their whole thought-life becomes vain and futile.

> *Because that, when they knew God, they glorified him not as God, neither were thankful;* ***but became vain in their imaginations, and their foolish heart was darkened****.* (Romans 1:21)

Another reason people turn their backs on God's offer of a full and free salvation is pride. The pride of the human heart is one of the terrible results of original sin. We would much rather *do* something to earn our salvation, so that we had something to boast about, than be a debtor to God's grace and mercy alone. This can be a particular problem for religious people who would rather trust in performing their church's various activities and rituals than simply trust in Christ's finished sacrifice for their sins.

Religion cannot save anyone, yet large numbers of modern churchgoers are deceived by their leaders into thinking that they will somehow be 'alright' in the end. Sadly, nothing could be further from the truth.

Another stumbling block for many is the existence of all the different world religions. Surely they cannot all be wrong, can they? Jesus said the following:

> *... I am **the** way, **the** truth, and **the** life: **no man** cometh unto the Father, **but by me**.* (John 14:6)

This is totally exclusive. He did not say that He was *a* way, but *the* way. The modern notion that all religions are just different paths to God does not stand up to even a cursory scrutiny. They are mutually contradictory and not one of them is able to deal with man's number one problem, sin. Their founders are dead and buried, never to be heard from again, whereas the tomb in which Jesus was laid is empty. The resurrection of Jesus Christ from the dead is a well-attested fact of history.

> *Neither is there salvation in any other: for **there is none other name** under heaven given among men, whereby we must be saved.* (Acts 4:12)

Time is fast running out for all of us. None of us know when our life will end, because God does not promise us tomorrow. Furthermore, the apocalyptic events that will end this present Age will commence suddenly, like a thief in the night. All indicators point to the likelihood that this will be well before the end of the natural lifespan of most readers.

Having read this far, if you have never before turned to God for His mercy and forgiveness of your sins, beware of putting it off until that fatal 'tomorrow'. It is a sobering truth that multitudes have entered Hell after dying in their sins, assuming that they always had 'tomorrow' to get right with God.

> *For he saith, I have heard thee in a time accepted, and in the day of salvation have I succoured thee: behold,* ***now*** *is the accepted time; behold,* ***now*** *is the day of salvation.* (2 Corinthians 6:2)

> *That if thou shalt* ***confess with thy mouth the Lord Jesus,*** *and shalt* ***believe in thine heart that God hath raised him from the dead, thou shalt be saved.*** (Romans 10:9)

> *For* ***whosoever shall call upon the name of the Lord shall be saved.*** (Romans 10:13)

APPENDIX 2

COMPARISON OF THE RAPTURE TO THE SECOND ADVENT

The Rapture		The Second Advent	
Christ comes ***to the air***	*1 Thessalonians 4:17*	Christ comes ***to the earth***	*Zechariah 14:4, Acts 1:11*
Christ comes ***for*** His saints	*1 Thes 4:16-17; Jn 14:2-3*	Christ comes ***with*** His saints	*1 Th 3:13; Jud14; Rev 19:14*
A mystery, unknown in the Old Testament	*1 Corinthians 15:51*	***Not a mystery*** Many OT prophecies	*Psalm 72, Isaiah 11 Zechariah 14 and others*
Not preceded by ***celestial signs*** or portents	*1 Thessalonians 5:1-3*	Heralded by ***many signs*** in the heavens	*Matthew 24:29-30 Luke 21:11,25-28*
A time of ***blessing***	*1 Thessalonians 4:18*	The Day of the Lord, ***darkness & judgment***	*Amos 5:18-20 2 Thessalonians 2:1-12*
Changed in twinkling of eye at Rapture, ***only His own see Him***	*1 Corinthians 15:51-52 1 Thessalonians 4:13-18*	***Every eye shall see Him*** Visible worldwide	*Matthew 24:27 Revelation 1:7*
Christ comes as the bright and morning star *(like Venus)*	*Revelation 22:16*	Comes as ***Sun*** of Righteousness with healing in His wings	*Malachi 4:2*
Those ***taken*** are for a ***blessing*** those ***left*** are for ***judgment***	*1 Thessalonians 4:13-18 1 Thessalonians 5:1-3 1 Thessalonians 5:9-10*	Those ***taken*** are for ***judgment*** those ***left*** are for a ***blessing*** in the Kingdom	*Matthew 24:37-41 Matthew 25:34-46*
No dating system for events preceding The Rapture		***Elaborate dating system*** - 1,260 days, 42 mths, 3½ yrs	*Daniel 7:25; 12:7,11-12 Revelation 11:2;12:14;13:5*
World is deceived afterwards by Satan through the man of sin	*2 Thessalonians 2:3-12*	Satan is bound so ***he can't deceive*** the nations	*Revelation 20:1-3*
Precedes the career of the man of sin	*2 Thessalonians 2:1-3*	***Terminates*** the career of the man of sin	*Revelation 19:20*
The Rapture seems to ***primarily*** involve ***The Church***	*John 14:1-4 1 Corinthians 15:51-58 1 Thessalonians 4:13-18*	End of Tribulation & Second Coming involves ***Israel primarily***, then Gentile nations	*Matthew chaps 24 & 25*
The title ***the Son of Man*** is ***never used*** in passages dealing with the Rapture		Second Coming is spoken of as ***the coming of the Son of Man***	*Matt 16:28; 24:27,30,39 Matthew 26:64 Mark 13:26; Luke 21:27*

Source documentation:

Believer's Bible Commentary *(2008)* by William MacDonald & biblestudytools.com